D1755993

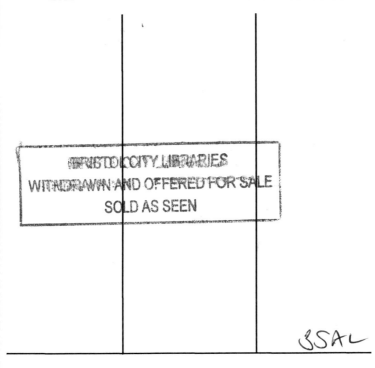
SSAL

Please return/renew this item by the last date shown
on this label, or on your self-service receipt.

To renew this item, visit **www.librarieswest.org.uk**
or contact your library

Your borrower number and PIN are required.

Libraries**West**

4 4 0174048   7

NECESSARY EVIL

Origins and Purpose

NECESSARY EVIL

Origins and Purpose

Hans-Werner Schroeder

Floris
Books

Translated by James H. Hindes

First published in German as *Der Mensch und das Böse*
by Verlag Urachhaus, Stuttgart in 1984
Abridged version first published in English by Floris Books, Edinburgh in 2005
This second edition 2022

British Library CIP Data available
ISBN 978-178250-801-4

Contents

Part Three — Destiny and Evil

Abbreviations after a biblical reference refer to the following translations:

JM — Jon Madsen, *The New Testament*

RSV — *Revised Standard Version*

JHH — James H. Hindes rendering of the author's German translation of the original Greek

Part One

Essence and Origin of Evil

Evil is hard to read about at times. Owing to current world events or even events in one's own life it would be understandable if the reader decided to put this book down halfway through. Yet, sometimes a difficult path must be followed for a long way before understanding and clarity emerge. The meaning of the whole, the reason for the journey, requires an overview possible only at the end.

The ideas presented in this book derive both from the work of Rudolf Steiner and from experiences with the renewed sacramental life of the Christian Community, Movement for Religious Renewal. I will refer often to both of these sources; for readers unfamiliar with them, a degree of openness will be helpful.

Those are my concerns about the reader's response to the idea presented here. The reason why I am handing this book over to be published are given in the first chapter. I hope my attempt to clarify these vital questions gives readers courage to face and engage with evil in whatever form it may present itself to them.

CHAPTER 1

Does Evil Have Any Meaning?

The existence of evil has always presented questions of many kinds. People have struggled to answer these questions since ancient times; proof of this effort is seen in the pictures found in the oldest myths, including the description of the 'Fall into sin' found in the Old Testament, as well as in the efforts of philosophers since ancient times, and in the thoughts of theologians even into the present. Nevertheless, to many these efforts are still unsatisfactory. Above all, the origin and meaning of evil have found no satisfactory explanation.

The unsolved riddle of evil

Even the great spirits such as Plato, Augustine, Thomas Aquinas and Schelling, to name but a few, arrive at solutions to the riddle of evil which are unsatisfactory to modern human beings. The appearance and effects of evil show themselves in the earthly realm, yet evil itself, in its essence, is of a spiritual nature; its origin lies in the realm of the spiritual. Every path of knowledge lacking direct insight into the conditions of the spiritual world must ultimately be powerless to answer these questions. Epistemological approaches, limited to the earthly world, can resort only to mere logical speculation. Philosophical and theological solutions since Plato are characterized by this shortcoming.

Before the beginning of philosophy in Greece in sixth century BC evil was portrayed in mythological pictures arising through ancient clairvoyance. To the extent that there were any statements about the origin of evil — usually its existence is simply presupposed — they are hardly sufficient for modern day consciousness and our need to understand. With today's intellectual approach to understanding we are rarely able to experience a picture deeply enough to be satisfied in the depths of our soul by its spiritual content, even with the most profoundly archetypal of mythological pictures. The situation was different for ancient, pre-conceptual modes of knowing (see Further Reading).

This holds true for statements concerning evil in the Old and New Testaments. In addition to the fact that evil is represented in the Bible by the Snake or the Dragon without any explanation of origin, the representation of evil — from the report of the Fall into sin described in Genesis to the fall of the dragon and other pictures in the Apocalypse — strikes us as richly mythological. Neither is there any 'systematic' presentation of evil which, in any case, could never provide an adequate explanation of evil by itself. This is evident from many theological attempts at explanation.

In early Christian times as well as in the Middle Ages it was enough for most people to feel the existence of a spiritual world in articles of faith, even though genuine vision and knowledge of the spiritual was long gone. At that time, it was a real comfort for many people lacking immediate insight into the spirit, simply to depend on faith in God's wisdom, omnipotence and goodness. It was not necessary to understand the origin and meaning of the powers of evil. Today, however, it is becoming increasingly necessary to shed light on the realm of evil because faith without knowledge is less and less possible, and because the threat posed by evil has reached hitherto unimaginable levels.

However, a longing for knowledge of the spiritual world as well as an ability to understand it is also growing. Paths to spiritual knowledge are again being sought today, and we might add they are open and can lead to knowledge of the spirit. For the first time in human history, the light of authentic spiritual knowledge can shine on the riddle of evil. This can also illuminate dark, mythic pictures from the past. The pictures from the Old and New Testaments can also be incorporated in a new and greater 'horizon of meaning.'

This book has come about through patient treading of the path of knowledge shown through the spiritual science of Rudolf Steiner. On this path it is possible to find inner certainty concerning the existence of the spiritual world and the spiritual beings found therein. New insights concerning evil also become possible. A conceptual foundation for such insights, which would justify them, cannot be attempted here; it would lead us too far afield. However, they can be found in anthroposophical literature (see Further Reading).

It is hoped that some of the ideas, which might at first appear dogmatic or improbable, will perhaps become more understandable and plausible when the book is seen as a whole. Many details from biblical traditions and theological dogma may appear in a different light when seen in this way.

Certain ideas commonly found in contemporary schools of theology, e.g. in the discussion of the Fall into sin, are omitted. This is not because I am unaware of these schools or do not value them, but because I am not concerned with the differences found in the various strata of historical documents, but rather with the comprehensive, meaningful picture of the world supporting the whole and superseding the many variations in the text. It is just this 'horizon of meaning' of the whole that creates a background giving individual details their meaning. That such an all-encompassing 'horizon of meaning' can be found all the way through the Bible has been shown repeatedly in the literature of the Christian Community (see Further Reading).

Today we need not be confounded by the riddle of evil. It is possible and necessary to take a step in the direction of understanding. My own experience in the realm of pastoral care has led me to undertake this book in the hope that it might be of some help to those who are struggling to understand evil as it confronts them in everyday life.

If evil exists, then God exists

Thomas Aquinas, the greatest thinker and theologian of Scholastic philosophy (thirteenth century) formulated these words: *Si malum est, Deus est* — If evil exists, then God exists.[1]

Such a statement was possible based on the epistemological presuppositions and progress of Thomistic philosophy. However, it is not easy for us today to accept such a formulation. Observing the current condition of humanity we would say: 'If evil exists today in mankind (and we certainly do experience it), then God is also at work in mankind.' In light of the horrors that humans perpetrate on one another it is not easy to make such a claim. Nevertheless, we must face this problem if we wish to investigate after the meaning of evil.

There is, however, one aspect of Thomas' statement that must make sense to us: that despite everything a peculiarly rich and varied relationship must exist between good and evil. For how could we recognize evil if there were no standard within us already that makes it possible to recognize evil when we see it? This standard could only be a fundamental knowledge or feeling for the good, which may not allow for full clarity in every instance, yet makes it possible for us to state categorically that evil does exist; there *are* destructive, threatening forces in the world. We need to protect ourselves and others from these forces. They make us fearful and raise deeply troubling and painful questions. This experience of evil is only possible because we also experience the good within us — just as the quality of darkness is possible only through the experience of light.

As Rudolf Steiner says:

> Unless there were something in us that goes beyond what we have already made of ourselves, then we would not be able to reprimand ourselves, neither would we be able to recognize ourselves. We must say: There is something living in us that is greater than what we have, up until now, made use of! If we transform such a judgment into a feeling, then we will look upon something that is known to us and which we can observe in our previous deeds and experiences; something that confronts us with the clarity that memory makes possible. And we will be able to compare that which has been revealed to us with something in our soul that is greater than what was revealed, with something that wants to emerge, with something that leads us to rise above ourselves and to judge ourselves from the standpoint of the present.[2]

The good makes its presence felt in us with this fundamental feeling described by Rudolf Steiner. To this extent we can connect the good to the divine, since the divine itself makes its presence felt in our humanity.

Therefore, for us today the quote from Thomas Aquinas could take the following form: 'Where we recognize and experience evil as evil, there the divine must also exist in us.'

A peculiar relationship and tension exists between good and evil. We have said that evil can only be recognized as evil because of our connection with good, but the opposite can also be the case. Grasping good *as good* even more deeply is the fruit of an encounter with evil. As long as we live only in good we do not truly know how to value it; we take it for granted. Only when we experience the contradiction between good and evil can we freely choose to stand on the side of good. We must therefore say: 'Only through the experience of evil can good be truly recognized,' or even more clearly, 'Good is only fully present and perceptible where evil was (or is) also present.'

These preliminary considerations allow us to surmise that a deeper meaning must be connected with the appearance of evil in humanity. We are, then, less amazed to discover that evil is not only radically described and defended against in the Old and New Testaments but that evil is, so to speak, even granted a place in world history. Cain, for example, is not killed by God but, as progenitor of his tribe, receives a special task. Judas is allowed into the circle of twelve disciples. The marriage parable found in Matthew 22 shows an invitation going out to both the good and the bad, and the adulteress in Chapter 8 of John's Gospel is not condemned by Christ, as is commanded in the Mosaic law.

CHAPTER 2

The Two Sides of Evil

We now turn to the basic fact concerning evil — it plays a double role. Apparently in ancient times it was believed that mankind's spiritual adversary appeared in two forms, not just one. For example, in Homer (800 BC), we have the picture of Scylla and Charybdis, which threaten Odysseus from two directions. (*Odyssey*, 12) Also the Chinese yin-yang philosophy appears originally to be based on this polarity. Later, however, this fact seems to have completely disappeared from humanity's consciousness. Neither in philosophy nor in theology of the last two thousand years years do we hear anything concerning this twofold aspect of evil. And neither does this fact have any role to play in more recent treatments of the question of evil — at least as far as I am aware.

The path of the golden mean

Its twofold nature is fundamental to an understanding of evil. We are indebted to Rudolf Steiner for knowledge of the two-sided essence of evil. In many contexts he pointed out that there is not only an opposition between good and evil in the world and in man, but above all an opposition between evil and evil, with good located between.[1]

One can most easily grasp this idea by considering certain virtues in the soul. Already Aristotle (around 300 BC) in the *Nicomachian Ethics* (2.2), showed that virtue always appears as the central point between two one-sided aberrations.

Seen this way, virtuous behaviour is caught between cowardice and recklessness; the proper way to handle money lies between greed and wasteful extravagance. The virtue of orderliness stands between pedantry and disorderliness, self-control between licentiousness and paralysing inhibition. A proper sense of self holds the middle ground between arrogance and self-disparagement; a healthy emotional state lies between effusive warmth and cold heartedness.

This fact is expressed in a beautiful way in the picture of the 'path of the golden mean' that runs through all these different forms of one-sidedness.

Once discovered, this perspective leads us to see opposites everywhere in the world and to find the middle or mean that belongs between them. This fundamental principle characterizes not only our soul life (which could be loosely defined as the contents of our psyche, both conscious and unconscious) but also our body and spirit. In our mental life we are threatened by the extremes of abstraction and fantasy. In the bodily part of our being we are threatened by asceticism and sensuality. True health lies in the middle between the dissolving (feverish) and hardening (sclerotic) tendencies in the body; every illness represents a deviation in one direction or the other away from a healthy balance of forces (see also Alfred Schütze's book, *The Enigma of Evil*). We see here a fundamental law of earthly life: there are forces at work here which would lead us in two directions towards one-sidedness. This would also include the masculine and feminine one-sidedness of the human condition.

Lucifer and Ahriman

Upon closer inspection it is possible to see the nature of the polarity revealed in the one-sidedness described above. This polarity lies behind, and is actually the basis for, all one-sidedness. Within us there is something at work that would lead us beyond ourselves and would magnify us in an illusory way. Recklessness, wasteful extravagance, disorderliness, licentiousness, arrogance, effusive warmth, fantasy, sensuality and fever are on this side. On the other side there is a drive to harden ourselves: cowardice, greed, pedantry, paralysing inhibition, feelings of worthlessness, cold heartedness, abstraction, asceticism, sclerosis.

On one side there is a striving to ignore the earthly and its necessities or to undervalue its importance. In its extreme form this ends in a complete escape from reality. On the other side we find a craving for the earth that can ultimately lead to loss of oneself to the earthly. These tendencies alternate in dominating the manic-depressive personality: mood swings between excessive optimism accompanied by a joyous celebration of life, and deep depression when it seems there is no hope whatsoever.

Let us list these one-sided opposites side by side:

> Recklessness — Cowardice
> Wasteful extravagance — Greed
> Disorderliness — Pedantry
> Licentiousness — Paralysing inhibition
> Arrogance — Feelings of inferiority
> Fantasy — Abstraction
> Sensuality — Asceticism
> Fever — Sclerosis
> Mania — Depression
> Flight from earth — Craving for the earth
> Dissolving Tendency — Ossifying Tendency

Now that we see these polarities clearly it may not be difficult to take the next step and recognize, in these one-sided extremes that play such an important role in human lives, not just 'forces' but actual *beings* who stand at our side and attempt to lead us astray in one direction or the other. There are two characteristically different errors and temptations that threaten us, between which we must constantly find our way. These are the two powers of evil, which we have to consider.

The fact that this truth has not yet been recognized in traditional forms of Christianity has been the cause of endless misunderstandings. 'Evil' has naively been placed over and against 'good' without regard for the fact that 'good' thereby slides easily towards the opposite one-sidedness. If one sees evil in a tendency towards the earth, in materialism, in craving for the earthly, then good must consist in a turning away from the earth, in a religiosity that denigrates the earthly. This kind of religion we know well enough, and not only in the Christianity of the Middle Ages; it sees earth as a vale of tears and heaven as paradise.

However, people then fall victim to the other one-sidedness without having found the middle, the balance between the two extremes. As we have seen, a 'good' striven for in this way is no good at all but rather a temptation; turning away from the earth cannot be an ideal for Christianity. The ideal must be sought in the middle, between earthly craving and earthly flight, in the possibility to stand on the earth without losing heaven, in the ability to turn to the spiritual in such a way that love for the earth is awakened.

Rudolf Steiner expressed this inner balance in the following verse:

> Seek the truly practical, material life,
> But seek it in such a way that it does not
> Numb your experience of the spirit that is active in that life.
> Seek the spirit, but do not seek it in
> Supersensible pleasure fed by supersensible egotism.
> But rather seek it because you want
> To apply it selflessly in a practical life in the material world.[2]

The beings that seek to pull us out of balance and onto their own paths are given two names in the spiritual science of Rudolf Steiner: Lucifer and Ahriman. These are spiritual beings. In his Letter to the Ephesians Paul says of them: 'We are not battling against flesh and blood ... but rather against spiritual powers of evil.' (6:12 JHH)

This fact opens to us knowledge essential to an understanding of evil. From what has been said already we can characterize the duality of these beings. *Lucifer* is the power that leads us out of ourselves, above ourselves, but who also entangles us in illusions and fantasies that can amount to escapism from the earth and its responsibilities. Selfishness and egotism are intimately connected with Lucifer's work. *Ahriman* is the power that tells us that physical, material existence alone is real, that earthly existence offers us true security and fulfilment in life. Ahriman produces sclerosis through cold, hard feelings and a craving for the earth, but also fear.[3]

The double role of evil

It is important to point out another fundamental fact about the two-sided nature of evil. 'Evil' does not always and everywhere bring about evil effects. 'Evil' can also produce something good in the right circumstances. A poison, when properly employed, can be used as a medication to heal. The dual nature of the adversary powers plays a double role in human existence and in the world. This means that they can bring about good or evil depending on other factors.

Re-examining the one-sided extremes listed above we see their dual value. They need not always be characterized as opposing good. For example, in certain situations it can be quite good to hold firmly to one's wallet and exercise 'moderated greed' when walking through a large department store (a bookstore might present a similar temptation for some people). In other situations it is right and proper to be extravagant with money. For example, it could be very good to be 'wasteful' with money when it comes to giving for the benefit of the needy.

There are forces in our soul that might provoke us to hang on to our money too tightly or to spend it extravagantly. We can make use of these forces to do what is right and proper, to do good. Corresponding examples could be given for other kinds of extreme one-sided attitudes listed above. Asceticism and sensuality also have a place in life where they serve good. These forces only become dangerous when we lose ourselves to them, when they rule us rather than serve us. Only then do they threaten our humanity. Within limits their activity is beneficial.

Luciferic forces are especially powerful in childhood and youth. Their activity in this age of life is entirely positive for they give freshness and enthusiasm lifting the child out of earth's heaviness. The hardening, 'depressing' Ahrimanic powers take hold of us in later years. They can help to create maturity and the wisdom that comes with time. Maturity and wisdom would not exist without these forces even though Ahrimanic powers are not directly responsible for them.

It is detrimental for a child to be exposed too early to the hardening, Ahrimanic forces that press us down towards the earth. Unfortunately this is not uncommon in many educational systems. Further along the road in the child's development severe difficulties will arise. An elderly man or woman, on the other hand, cannot simply return to a childlike attitude towards life. The carefree naiveté of a child would not be appropriate for someone advanced in years. The well known biblical quote from Matthew 18:3, 'Unless you become like little children you will not enter the kingdom of Heaven,' (JHH) does not contradict this. The words mean that the soul qualities which a child possesses *naturally* must be acquired again by adults on a higher level *consciously*, if they are to have access to spiritual reality. The ability to feel wonder and amazement, devotion, uncomplicated openness to other human beings and a natural love for all that surrounds the child are virtues when they occur in adults.

Ahrimanic and Luciferic powers can exert a beneficial influence when they appear at the proper time. As can be seen, it is not an unreasonable speculation that the forces of evil can have a meaningful role to play. Something that can bring about evil can *also* produce something good when it occurs in the proper situation, at the right 'location.' In other words: Evil is a Good occurring at the wrong place and/or at the wrong time. Just as fire is good and useful in its proper place but destructive when it breaks through its boundaries, so too are the effects of evil.

The two-sided nature of evil can also be seen in history. In the past, 'at the proper place,' Luciferic powers have made an enormous contribution to humanity's development. Above all they are responsible for calling forth our quest for knowledge and artistic creation. Knowledge and art are gifts from Lucifer.[4]

This is easy to see for artistic activity. Where would art be if we did not have the ability and the impulse to lift ourselves up, and free ourselves from earthly facts and reality? The child is already an unconscious artist in his play and fantasy life. The gift of Lucifer is at work here in a way that enriches human life enormously.

What about knowledge? If we consider the question of the child's desire to know, we are confronted with the starting point of all knowledge: the Luciferic desire to go beyond the immediately given, to find out what stands behind or '*under*' appearances, to '*under*stand' the immediately given. This can be seen at the beginning of the Old Testament. Lucifer tempts Adam and Eve to eat from the tree of knowledge. This has a positive side also. Could someone, who was not able to distinguish between good and evil, even be called a human being? There is a reason why the name Lucifer means 'light bringer' in Latin. Mankind is indebted to him for his luminous gifts. However, these are gifts that can also shine a false light, the superficial light of mere appearance; this light then becomes a danger to human beings.

Ahriman also has his positive significance for humanity. He must see to it that mankind has an interest in the earth (Lucifer in a sense does exactly the opposite). He makes sure that man works the earth 'in the sweat of his brow' and acquires the ability not only to create a world of beautiful appearances (in art) but also to create, with the help of technology, a magnificent, sturdy and tangible kingdom of earthly usefulness.

That it is really Ahriman who is at work here is made abundantly clear by the destructive effects of our technological civilization. The name 'Ahriman' is derived from the Persian, *Angra mainyu*, and means 'evil spirit.' The essence of evil as cold destructiveness is fully revealed in him.

World contradictions

Both Adversaries have a great, encompassing significance for human-ity. We get a better idea of this if we consider their work in the natural world at large. Although we first considered their effects in the human world they also come to meet us in the larger context of the universe as cosmic beings and forces. They participate in the formation of all earthly life including the earth itself.

We recognize the effects of Ahriman's work in everything that makes the earth hard, that produces gravity and binds things to the earth. In contrast to this, forces of 'levity' and dissolution work from peripheral, cosmic heights. The further we distance ourselves from the surface of the earth the less we are dealing with matter. These forces of levity, streaming in from the periphery, make it possible for plants to grow upwards *against* gravity, and are physically effective as cen-trifugal forces.

Life in the kingdoms of nature unfolds *between* these forces; with-out them nature could not exist and would immediately come to an end if only one of them were to exert its influence.

The opposing forces of hot and cold are obvious. We experience in cold the forces that call forth contraction and rigidity, in heat the expanding and dissolving forces. A similar polarity lives in light and darkness.

These facts belong to the natural order. However, when we see that they are really only part of a higher order, then we see how these one-sided extremes serve the beneficial working of nature in a wonderful way.

One can ask the question: Was that always the case? Or was there perhaps, in earlier stages of earthly evolution, a phase, in which this order in nature, which we take for granted, had first to be created? Is perhaps the integration of the Adversaries into the creation of the world a cosmic deed that was preceded by a struggle involving those spiritual beings responsible for the creation of the world? And is this struggle continuing today within the soul of man?

We see here, at the outset, that when the Adversaries are subject to a higher lawfulness their activity serves good. As forces at work in the physical world we have also seen that they occupy a mighty position in the kingdoms of nature. Something of their adversarial majesty can perhaps become clear to us when we consider that they are active, not only in the human realm but are also an intrinsic part of the whole of creation.

Let it be mentioned here in passing that the East-West polarity of mankind also manifests the all-encompassing character of these polar forces.[5]

The mean

In nature the one-sided extremes of gravity and 'levity,' light and darkness, heat and cold, day and night, all serve the mean — a middle place where life on earth is possible. This middle place is also present in plants, animals and man and, finding freedom in a balance between these extremes, it develops life *between and with* the help of these opposites. The mean is not firmly fixed; it has a pulsating quality of life; it looks different in winter than in summer, in the morning than in the evening.

With a royal sovereignty, so to speak, nature makes use of these opposites for her own purposes in order to manifest herself with rich variety. Nature with all her living complexities does not appear because opposites are present (a mechanistic, Ahrimanic thought), but rather opposites are present in order to make the richness of life on earth possible.

Can we say something similar about human beings? One-sided extremes are fully present in us but we must struggle daily for our 'middle,' for the development of our full humanity. It is not simply 'fixed in place' but must ever be found anew.

We have already seen this in our relationship to money. It is not possible to simply say: 'one must handle money in this or that way,' for at certain times 'reasonable greed,' or 'generous wastefulness' may be in order. Good is recreated only with a wakeful presence of mind.

In this we see the actual greatness and freedom of what it means to be human. Good must be created by us. The two Adversaries at our side call forth the crucial middle within us by constantly putting it into question. Our essential humanity can only be developed by living between spirit and matter in a life as rich and manifold as the life of nature, which is also formed between heaven and earth. Friedrich Schiller expressed something of this secret in his book *On the Aesthetic Education of Man, in a Series of Letters*. He presents the idea that man experiences 'necessity' from two sides: 'the necessity of nature' and 'the necessity of reason,' when the 'sense-drive' exerts force on us physically and the 'form-drive' compels us morally (14th Letter). Schiller shows how man can dissolve and balance these one-sided extremes and necessities through a middle element which he calls 'the drive to play' referring to the artistic process of creation. This 'play-drive' is a higher, third element that can integrate the opposites.

We have seen that Lucifer and Ahriman stand as beings behind the one-sided extremes of nature. Is there perhaps someone, a being, who guards over the mean, the middle, who watches over the sensitive interaction between the opposites that takes place in that region of the human soul where the essence of our humanity is gradually being created?

With this question we touch on the mystery of Christ. At this point we would like merely to point to a picture in the gospel. We read there: 'they crucified him and with him two others, one on the one side, the other on the other side, and Jesus in the middle.' (John 19:18 JM)

CHAPTER 3

The Devil's Golden Hair — Evil in Fairy Tales

Human experiences of evil in ancient times find expression in mythological images. The pictures and myths concerning evil originated at a time in which clairvoyance was still very much alive and strong. We must conclude that human beings' capacity for knowledge was actually opened more to the spiritual world and its beings, than to the physical, sensory world. They actually saw into the spiritual world all around them.

The information that has come down to us about the spiritual world and its beings is pictorial, not conceptual, in character. The 'gods,' good and evil nature spirits, 'demons,' 'angels,' etc. are pictures of spiritual beings found in old myths, sagas and epic stories.

These pictures are extraordinarily manifold, variable and alive. We can imagine that clairvoyant sight at that time penetrated into a mighty world of images. These pictures did not have the formed and stationary character we are familiar with in the physical world. Our picture of a tree in the physical world does not metamorphose into anything else; it remains itself, a tree. The world of images available to spiritual sight was entirely alive, flowing and filled with movement.

The two figures of the adversary powers appear on this level of reality, the level of the spiritual world, presented in many different images with various names: as snake or dragon or wolf; Scylla and Charybdis; devil and Satan; Lucifer and Ahriman; Behemoth and Leviathan, etc.[1]

In addition to this realm of myths portraying evil there is the realm of fairy tales which is easier to understand yet contains great depth and wisdom. Fairy tales do not arise from any arbitrary folk-fantasy. Simply the fact that the same significant motifs reoccur in a similar way in different ethnic groups can save us from this misapprehension. The actual source of fairy tales is found in wisdom that was based originally on dream-like or clairvoyant, insights into the spiritual world. This wisdom streamed into the souls of storytellers and bards as a force that could create images.[2] Variations in the motifs can be ascribed to the image-creating power of storytellers working in different ways in different ethnic groups. This power must not be thought of as arising out of the arbitrary will of the storyteller. The variations show us different valid aspects and levels of the motifs.

With this understanding of genuine fairy tales we will not be surprised to find deep wisdom in them with respect to the workings of evil. Evil appears in fairy tales in manifold forms: as witch and sorcerer, as the devil and the devil's grandmother, as wolf and dragon (as well as other animal forms), as the evil stepmother and evil fairy, also as nature spirits inimical to human beings: goblins, dwarfs, giants, elves and trolls.

It is perhaps startling how evil appears in fairy tales: it is simply there as a matter of course! Its origin is not explained, not even inquired after; its existence is accepted without question. Fairy tales give us no information concerning the origin of evil but tell us all the more about its significance for human life and destiny.

Most fairy tales become meaningful only when evil appears. Without evil the plot would not develop, would not even get started; everything would remain 'as of old' if evil did not bring about dangers, trials, temptations, errors and enchantment. Fairy tales show us evil as an essential element in life, despite which life goes on.

This positive view of evil is the reason why children can handle without any problem the so-called gruesome pictures of fairy tales. Children feel instinctively that fairy tales point to a higher reality in which good and evil have their appropriate places. In fairy tales they experience the superiority of good over evil.

The attraction of evil — the ethic of the path

Fairy tales have a vivid relationship to evil. As with myths we find in fairy tales that the good is in no way 'normal.' It must be found ever anew as the middle between two extremes.

'The ethic represented in fairy tales is an ethic of the path, the way.'[3] This means not only that the encounter with evil initiates an inner path but also that movement is called forth leading to the overcoming of evil. 'Acting spontaneously, the hero engages himself both with the situation at hand and the achievement of a goal. This activity is not merely good; its virtue is that it enables the hero to stay on the "path," on the way to the goal.'[4] Fairy tales do not preach any specific system of morality; they describe the human power to take initiative that comes from the heart. This power is always ready to take action even in the most difficult situations. And even if it does not at first succeed, in the end it finds the right path.

An extreme example of this is seen in Grimm's tale of the Frog Prince, where the king's daughter, precisely in not doing good, in performing what is apparently an act of childish spite, throws the frog against the wall and thereby brings about salvation for the prince. If the princess had not followed the spontaneous impulse of her heart the prince would have had to remain eternally enchanted as a frog.

Of course, spontaneous impulses do not always lead to good. Snow White follows the temptations of the evil queen and is led into a life-threatening situation. Little Red Riding Hood leaves the path and is then eaten by the wolf. Both of these figures could only be saved by other forces 'from outside' — through the prince, the dwarfs, the hunter.

The ability to arrive at a good and proper goal is developed through *experience*, through the painful experience that results from engaging soul-forces that are *also* capable of going astray.

Transformation

Exploring further the path aspect of fairy tales we see that the encounter with evil always brings about a transformation:
1. through courage and initiative shown in tests and dangers;
2. through enduring suffering and death;
3. as salvation of something on a lower level of existence.

In the first case we see a 'hero' who can also be a 'stupid fool,' a neglected 'youngest son or daughter,' etc. who then, through bravely enduring an ordeal and dangers, attains the hand of the king's daughter and then becomes king himself. The resistance provided by evil powers usually plays a decisive roll. The result shows clearly that the hero has not only travelled an external path but was able to achieve an elevation, or intensification of his soul-forces through his engagement with evil. The picture, the archetype of the king is an expression or a symbol of the fact that someone has attained his (or her!) full humanity, that can only be acquired by passing many tests and ordeals. At the end of the path the hero is transformed and elevated in an essential way.

In the second case inner transformation is achieved through the suffering that evil brings. 'Hansel and Gretel' is an example of this. The children enter the realm of evil, which they are able to overcome after they have experienced it. A fundamental change occurs, for the witch is no more. We find similar motifs in 'The Wolf and the Seven Kids,' and 'The Juniper Tree.'

The third case is the most mysterious. Something that is of a lower order conceals within itself something higher and is then transformed, redeemed. One evocative picture of this is the bear in the fairy tale of 'Snow White and Rose Red.' Hidden in the bear is a prince who can be saved. Because the girls do not simply avoid the creepiness of the bear they are able to participate in the higher salvation the bear undergoes when the prince is 'dis-enchanted.'

The third kind of transformation contains something even deeper. To begin with, we see that something higher is 'enchanted' in something lower. This higher element wants to be saved and can be. What if every 'lower' being, even evil itself, contained something higher that was 'enchanted' within it? What if this higher being could be redeemed if only mankind had the right attitude towards it? It is not difficult to see how these motifs are related to human life. The last motif, salvation, points to higher forces in our life; here we touch on the essential mysteries of Christianity, which will be considered later in the book.

The good in evil

There is yet another motif that takes us further. It is seen in its archetypical form in the fairy tale 'The Devil with whe Three Golden Hairs.' Imagine that the devil can have *golden* hair. This picture does not stand alone; in a slightly different form it appears when the devil (or a dragon, etc.) guards a treasure, possesses the king's daughter, or possesses knowledge that can help people, and that can be conveyed only by the devil or dragon himself.

What does all this mean? Nothing more and nothing less than that there is something precious in the 'realm,' and possession of, evil, something that must be acquired by human beings through their encounter with evil. Only the 'Devil with the golden hair' knows what is good in time of need, he has a certain knowledge of what is good and helpful and this knowledge must be wrestled from him. In the struggle with evil something must be acquired that evil alone can give.

When we spoke about the 'double role' of evil we saw that good in evil only shows itself when evil is properly 'handled' by man. This motif is seen in its classical form in the Siegfried saga: Siegfried kills the dragon and wins the treasure that the dragon had protected. By bathing in the blood of the dragon he becomes invulnerable to wounds in battle (except for the place on his back where a linden tree leaf fell and prevented the blood from touching his skin). Finally a drop of dragon blood is squirted onto his tongue which allows him to understand the language of the birds. Siegfried acquires the treasure, invulnerability and a deeper knowledge of nature, from the dragon.

The fairy tale of 'The King's Son and the Devil's Daughter' goes even further. We quote again from Verena Kast's book *Witches, Ogres and The Devil's Daughter*:

> In fairy tales, the existence of evil is taken for granted. In
> this, they convey the idea that where there is evil, there is also
> always hope. One need only take the right approach. The tale
> of the king's son and the devil's daughter is a good example.
> Though evil is present, embodied by the devil, at the same time
> and in the same house, we have his daughter, who helps to
> overcome evil (who is actually her own father). (p. 38)

We find within evil itself the very power we need to overcome it. Perhaps there is more in this picture, for the fact that the devil can have a daughter would suggest that there are forces in evil that have a future. Does this perhaps promise a future for good?

Our brief look at the wisdom in fairy tales has given us seven fundamental motifs:
— Evil is accepted, not complained about.
— Without it nothing gets started.
— Good is developed through evil.
— Transformation is possible through courageous actions in the face of evil.
— Transformation is possible through enduring suffering.
— Transformation is possible through powers of redemption.
— Precious treasures can lie hidden in evil.

That the devil can even have a daughter who unites herself with good is a further motif that points to the future.

It is important to note that there are a few fairy tales in which evil cannot be overcome, but must be escaped, for example the eerie tale of Bluebeard. Here it is clear that human strength is not sufficient for a positive outcome in the encounter with every form of evil. And not every devil has a golden hair. There are forms of evil that we must not touch, that are too dangerous for us. This too is in the wisdom of fairy tales — and in life itself. Perhaps there is a task in the future for mankind in dealing with evil, a task for which our powers are not yet sufficient.

CHAPTER 4

The World of Angels

When looking at Adversaries and evil it is easy to become fascinated by what we see. For this reason, we must not forget that there is also a world of 'good' with its beings and deeds. By considering this world of good we will acquire a further point of view for understanding evil, and a first answer to the question of the origin of evil.[1]

From angels to Seraphim

The kingdoms of nature display a simple order for their wealth of phenomena. First there is the trinity of minerals, plants and animals. Within this threefoldness we can see a rich differentiation of characteristics and connections. It is part of Christian tradition to see not only a natural order *below* man, but also an order above man, a so-called hierarchy of spiritual beings that is no less rich in its fullness and detail than the natural order. This tradition goes back to Dionysius the Areopagite, a disciple of Paul's.[2] It is also found in Paul's letters although not systematically developed. We can assume that in much earlier times there was a widespread awareness of angelic hierarchies connected with ancient mystery knowledge. The existence of such beings standing above man is taken for granted in the mythologies of all nations, as well as in the Old and New Testaments. There is also an organization of various individual beings according to their different tasks and realms of activity.

Anthroposophy makes it possible for us to take such descriptions seriously again. In the renewed Christian rituals, in the sacraments of the Christian Community, the existence of the realms of angels is realized and actualized in many ways. For example, during the twelve days of Christmas the names of the nine kingdoms of angels are invoked in the Act of Consecration of Man (the name for the Eucharist, the mass in the Christian Community).

Those beings standing closest to us in the hierarchies are the *Angels*, *Archangels* and Archai (also called spirits of time).

— *Angels* are the guardian spirits and the 'genius' of individual humans. They lead people through earthly and spiritual existence and are active in the formation and guidance of human destiny.

— *Archangels* stand one stage higher, they are one step more powerful than angels. They do not guide individual humans but rather groups of people, indeed entire peoples or nations. They are the leaders of ethnic groups, countries and are the inspirational spirits of language.

— *Archai* are again one stage higher and permeate all humanity with their forces. They are the spirits who guide the destiny and progress of all humanity and inspire the various ages of history.

This lowest trinity of angelic beings is also called the **third hierarchy**.

As a further group of three we find the **second hierarchy**, whose members are the *Exusiai*, (also known as Revealers or Spirits of Form), *Dynameis* (also known as World Powers or Spirits of Movement) and *Kyriotetes* (also known as World Guides or Spirits of Wisdom). They are not directly concerned with shaping or influencing the conditions of an individual human or humanity as a whole, but are active as the forces informing and shaping the earth and the cosmos.

— *Exusiai* are the creators of forms and shapes on earth, both in large and small. Thus their name, according to Rudolf Steiner, 'Spirits of Form' (*exusiai* in Greek means 'might' or 'power ').

— *Dynameis* see to it that in addition to there being forms in the world, there is also movement, alteration and change in appearances in space and time. For this reason they are called 'Spirits of Movement' (in Greek *dynameis* means 'force'— from it we derive the word 'dynamic').

— *Kyriotetes* make possible the harmony and wisdom-filled inner connectedness of everything that happens in the world. Hence, they are called the 'Spirits of Wisdom' (in Greek *kyrios* means Lord; *kyriotes* means rulership and *kyriotetes* is the plural form).

Above this second hierarchy is the **first hierarchy** consisting of *Thrones*, *Cherubim*, and *Seraphim*. We are able perhaps to form some idea of the working of the second and third hierarchies; understanding the first hierarchy is, however, more difficult. Here we are dealing with spiritual powers who have created not only the *form* of the world, but above all the substance of the world. From their substance the being and substance of the world has come forth through their working together with the highest Godhead.[3]

— *Thrones* are also called 'Spirits of Will.' This name is a telling expression of the fact that they stand very close to the Godhead, as if they were resting in the Godhead like a throne. The name given them by spiritual science — 'Spirits of Will' — is a reminder that their sacrificial will is performing the will of God. The world arose through the willed sacrifice of their own being.

— *Cherubim* appear (as do the Seraphim) in the Old Testament, standing in the direct presence of God. As the spirits of harmony they point to the foundation and goal of all creation: the harmony of all beings (*Cherub* in Hebrew, *cherubim* is the plural, so too *seraph, seraphim*).

— *Seraphim* are the highest beings. They are called 'Spirits of Love' and, as such, witness the fact that love streams forth directly from God. They occupy the highest level of world creation.

With this brief look into 'the world of good,' i.e. the beings that bear the creative forces of goodness in the world, we have had space to touch on only an outline of their true nature.

The highest God and 'the gods'

Above the Seraphim, we find the highest divinity, the Trinity. But we must not forget that at the same time the essence of God permeates everything; it is not just sitting on a throne in a state of pure other-worldliness, detached from reality.

The theological objection brought against the one-sidedness of Pantheism (that God has been 'poured out' into the world) is certainly justified. God, as the 'entirely other' should not simply be identified with the world. However, this fact must not lead to the other extreme of denying that he is active with, in and through all the different creatures in the world.

This is especially true for the work of Christ, who, as the Son, has descended from the greatest heights down through the spheres of nine realms of angels to unite with mankind; Paul says of him that 'all exists in him' (Col.1:17 JHH)

Just as the soul and spirit of man permeate the body without becoming identical to it, so too God permeates the various regions and beings of creation, including the realms of the angels that have come forth directly from him.

What then is the 'rank' of the 'gods' in pre-Christian religions and mythologies? It is not difficult to see that pagan divinities do not originate in the very highest levels of the spiritual world. The old Norse gods of the Germanic peoples are themselves subject to the voice of destiny from the Norns. They knew they lived their lives in the 'twilight of the gods.' The generations of Greek gods with their eventful destinies are often very close to human beings, even situated in the 'human, all too human.' Marduk, the Babylonian god, can be identified as the dragon slayer along with Michael the archangel, which would make him a being with the rank of an archangel.

In pre-Christian mythologies, in general, we are dealing with beings that can be characterized as angels and archangels. These are the beings standing closest to the human and were therefore the easiest for clairvoyants of that time to see. They were also the most important beings for human destiny.

We find in all mythologies that speak of 'gods' the surprising fact that gods also have destinies. That is, we find development and transformation in a region to which we would normally ascribe eternal being and unchanging perfection. We have already seen this in the realm of the adversary powers. There is, in the world of spiritual beings, evolution and development. Indeed, the closer any spiritual region is to the world of humans the more likely transformation will be found there. Development means to unfold something in oneself that up until now was not unfolded or developed; it means to be able to ascend, but perhaps also to remain behind. Mankind has a central place and special significance in this everywhere present process.

The place of Adversaries

Right at the beginning of the Book of Job, one of the greatest books in the Old Testament, we encounter a shocking statement: 'Now there was a day when the sons of God came to present themselves before the Lord and Satan also came among them' (Job 1:6 RSV) Satan among the 'sons of God' means to be among the angels. Further along we even hear that the Lord considers Satan worthy to hold a conversation with him. The Lord inquires about what Satan has been doing and then directs his attention to a man named Job. If we were not so accustomed to the picture that occurs in the twelfth chapter of the Book of Revelation, it too, would amaze us: the dragon in heaven!? How did he get there? What is he supposed to do there? ('the accuser of our brethren day and night' Rev.12:10). How long has he been there? Satan among the sons of God, the dragon in heaven? Where is the place of evil?

There was already a tradition in Judaism that evil could be traced back to angelic powers who, out of pride, had risen up in rebellion against God and for that reason had been cast down. Satan, or Lucifer, as a fallen angel is a theme found in Jewish Apocryphal literature especially in the time just before the appearance of Christ. Above all, the *Book of Enoch* is concerned with this question. It enjoyed much renown in the first age of Christianity and is probably the source of the early Church fathers' view that it was the sin of angels and their resulting fall (which is not found in the Bible) that led to man's Fall.

The Adversaries originally belonged to the kingdom of angels. If it is true that the Adversaries were among the powers that created the world, then they must have originated at least from the level of the second hierarchy, if not from the periphery of the first hierarchy.

Thus the essence of the adversary stands before us, powerful and awe-inspiring. All the more pressing then is the question: how and when did evil come about?

CHAPTER 5

An Attempt to Understand
the Origin of Evil

We have seen already a basic concept for understanding the origin of evil: the double role of evil. Evil shows itself as a good that has been shifted, has become one-sided, is no longer in harmony or has lost its original place. This thought has occurred to philosophers in the past.[1] This development has also occurred in the mythological image of evil, e.g. the dragon had to *become* evil; at first it represented something good. Good beings can become evil when they are active at the wrong place at the wrong time.

In the human realm, sexuality can serve as an example, or egotism, for without a degree of egotism no one can live (we must have food, shelter and clothing for ourselves to begin with. But devotion and selflessness must eventually come to supplement egotism to establish a balance; otherwise what is positive and necessary for us becomes pernicious and destructive.

In the second of his Mystery Dramas Rudolf Steiner portrays this idea in pictorial form in his story of 'The Man With An Axe.' The story goes:

> Once there was a man who thought a great deal about the world. He was most tortured by the question of the origin of evil. He could not account for it. 'The world is from God,' he said to himself, 'and God can only have goodness in him. How do evil people come from the good?' Again and again he considered this in vain. The answer could not be found. One day while walking on his way our thinker saw a tree that was having a conversation with an axe. The axe said to the tree, 'I can do what you are unable to do, I can fell you down.' Then the tree said to the vain axe, 'A year ago a man took wood and out of my wood made your handle with another axe.' And as the

man heard the conversation a thought took root in his mind that he was unable to express clearly in words. Yet it gave him a full answer to the question: How can evil come from the good?[2]

Expressed in conceptual form this story says: Something taken out of a living context and made independent can, in the next moment, turn and prove destructive to this context.

Beings who have stayed behind

We need to grasp this thought more concretely; for we are dealing not only with 'powers' that have been 'displaced' and have fallen out of their proper context but with beings that belonged to the world of angels.

The world evolves constantly. All beings, not just human beings, participate in this progress. In particular, it is the angels of the third and second hierarchies that mature as they develop their unique capacities through their creative activity. Meanwhile, in the first hierarchy (Seraphim, Cherubim, and Thrones) a blessed devotion to creation holds sway.

On this path of advancing evolution some beings can 'stay back' or, in a sense, be 'deferred.' When that happens they drop out of the normal progression of creation. This creates an irregularity, a disturbance. Rudolf Steiner speaks of this impediment occurring even among higher angelic beings during the evolution of the universe.

But 'staying behind' is not as simple as grades in a school where, if a pupil fails a year, he simply joins the class a year behind and then learns the content missed the first time. For the angels in the next lower 'class' have entirely different strengths and tasks than those angels standing above them.

So the hindered beings are displaced; they are held back one 'world grade,' so to speak. Yet because they are so different, they are unable to establish contact with these lower-standing beings, who for their part have an entirely different impulse and orientation with the world. So these beings must continue working, so to speak, but now in the wrong place, just as they worked before in the correct place that corresponded to their constitutional predisposition. Meanwhile, the normal course of world evolution continues.

Since these beings cannot simply disappear but must continue working, they seek opportunities to work with other beings that stand further below them. In this way, they bring something 'out of season' and destructive into the evolution of the world, particularly in the human realm which, as we will see, actually becomes their preferred stage.

A starting place for understanding the origin of evil is given to us with the concepts of 'remaining behind,' 'falling out of evolution' and 'displacement.' But the question arises: how does such 'remaining behind' happen?

Directive from God — the sacrifice of angelic beings

The concept of 'remaining behind' or impediment is easily understood as a failure, as though the hindered beings' 'declassification' was due to their weakness or negligence. Already the question of how something like this could ever happen in the spiritual world, which is permeated by divine beings, leads us to doubt we are on the right track. A teacher who is properly connected with her pupils will do everything possible to prevent any one of them from having to remain behind. How much more is it then within the power of God to prevent angelic beings from remaining behind?

We need two additional concepts to add to our understanding of 'angelic deferment:' *divine guidance* and *angelic sacrifice*.

The angels remained behind, especially the higher, leading angelic beings, not out of weakness or guilt; it was connected with divine guidance.[3] Just as a military strategist, for example a general, sometimes assigns specific missions to special units of troops — which can sometimes involve remaining behind, even long isolation or independence — so God did with respect to the 'heavenly hosts.' He separated hierarchical beings from himself and set them free to go their own way, and thereby to undertake special tasks necessary to the evolution of the world.

This certainly involved a difficult sacrifice.[4] It must have meant the greatest pain and suffering for those beings to be separated from the immediate presence of God, to no longer participate in divine creation. The ancient philosophical view that evil is nothing more than a kind of void or absence of the divine could be understood as this exclusion from creative activity. Good alone is creative; evil itself leads to nothingness, to emptiness, into separation from God. This does not mean that the Adversaries are not completely real, but that they are not actually *creative* in the sense of world evolution.

The concept of sacrifice (if one is allowed to use any human concept) is most appropriate to describe the deferment of spiritual beings. Just as a human being may take on pain for the sake of a greater necessity, so did the hierarchal beings. In the realm of the higher beings who took this sacrifice upon themselves the high, divine meaning of the sacrifice must have been clear to them for a time; only later perhaps did they lose sight of this meaning. At first they followed divine guidance out of an insight into world necessity.

It was divine guidance and sacrifice then that first brought about the holding back of these beings. For, we must say, how could a being that experienced the blessing closeness to the divine, distance itself or even want to distance itself, if this willingness did not at first lie in the will of God? The self-willing that belongs to freedom could only be possible at a distance from God.

Hence, there is nothing original in the constantly asserted self-will of the Adversaries, which is supposed to have led to the Fall. For in the presence of God there was simply no place for such self-will and freedom. The Godhead is too great, too overwhelming in its goodness and power. In its presence nothing is possible other than devotion to this goodness and the will to serve the divine.

The thought of rebelling against divine omnipotence, the wish to turn against divine goodness can only originate in a state of being far from God. Hence, a distancing from the divine must have preceded the rebellion. A certain element of freedom begins to work in these retarded beings. They are on their own. That also means the appearance of egotism, of being oneself, of wanting to be oneself, that did not exist until then in the hierarchies. Because these beings were no longer guided by the Godhead, they were 'left to their own devices,' that is they were in a certain way 'free' from divine guidance. They had to use their own guidance to develop and decide how they would work into the world. However, this was exactly what was necessary for the progression of God's plan for the world.

Rejection, abstention and renouncement

What did it mean for the other hierarchal beings that brothers from their ranks were separated and remained behind?

Rudolf Steiner describes how the Thrones (the lowest level of the first hierarchy) are deeply devoted to the Cherubim who work just above them, that they sacrifice in pure devotion the best forces of their being to these spirits who stand high above them. This fact appears to spiritual sight in a mighty picture: The Thrones, united also with the Kyriotetes, the spirits of wisdom, are devoted to the Cherubim in sacrificial activity. Their sacrifice appears as a glowing offering and as smoke rising from that offering. It is received by the Cherubim and taken up to be transformed into creative forces.

Now some of these sacrificing beings are to remain behind. That means that the offering and the taking up, the blessedness of both the sacrifice and the receiving must be interrupted. Some of the Cherubim forego the substance offered by the Thrones; they reject the offering. 'In this picture we have the sacrificing Thrones and the Cherubim who accept the sacrifice; we also have some Cherubim who do not accept the sacrifice but give back what reaches them as an offering.' Thus wrote Rudolf Steiner, whose pronouncements on these events we will be quoting in the following paragraphs.[5]

In this way the coherence of the hierarchies was interrupted. The interactions of spiritual beings simply did not continue. A rejection from the side of the highest angelic beings occurred. As a result, the beings directly beneath them remain standing, stopped in their development because an exclusion from further evolution is implicit in the rejection.

This no doubt meant great pain for those left behind. But this rejection also meant 'doing without' for the Cherubim, the angelic beings doing the rejecting. For they lost substances and forces (every true sacrifice represents substance and force) that were essential for their work.

Resignation and a sacrifice were required not only of the rejected and therefore impeded beings, but also from the others. This thought is required to supplement the motif of sacrifice belonging to the deferred angels. A feeling of loss and resignation must have gone through the realms of angels when these angelic beings were separated from the rest. It was a feeling of incompleteness; a feeling that something was missing due to the loss of their companions on the journey. But there is a positive aspect to this loss. Even with humans, strength can be increased by painful resignation. The power of the Cherubim was intensified by the suffering they endured.

If we follow the experience of these beings a little further, we find something entirely new in world evolution.

> If the Cherubim had accepted the sacrifice, then the Luciferic
> beings could not have been left behind ... In order for it to
> be possible for beings to become independent in this way, a
> renunciation, a foregoing had to precede. It was so ordered
> by divine providence that the gods [Steiner means here the
> higher hierarchal beings] called forth their own Adversaries.
> If the gods had not foregone the offerings from below, then
> the lower beings could not have opposed them. Or expressed
> more prosaically, we could say that the gods had looked ahead
> and realized: 'If we keep going in this way ... beings will
> never arise who are able to act freely out of their own personal
> impulses. For such beings to arise we must create the possibility
> for Adversaries to arise in the universe who oppose us ... If
> we alone order everything we would not be able to find such
> opposition. We could make everything very easy for ourselves
> by accepting all sacrifices, then all evolution would be subject
> to us. But we won't do that; we want beings who are free from
> us, who can oppose us.'[6]

These words indicate how the power of freedom, of independence, comes about in cosmic evolution. They also describe how the power of opposition begins to work in the universe.

> We will find it easy to understand that ... the substance of
> will, which the Thrones actually wanted to sacrifice to higher
> spiritual beings, had to remain back in the Thrones who wanted
> to sacrifice and couldn't ... that the beings who wanted to bring
> an offering had to create a mood within themselves. We can
> feel that with this mood something begins, which is, even if
> extraordinarily gentle, an opposition to the beings who rejected
> the offering.

At the beginning, this power of opposition stirs as a gentle enmity against the higher beings.

> We can call these beings: *beings with suppressed will*. Through
> the fact that they had to have this suppressed will within
> they were in a very special situation ... Can you not feel how
> something shoots in there that can be called 'egohood' and
> then later comes out as egotism in all its forms. Viewed in
> this way one can feel what then later poured, so to speak, into
> evolution, lives on as an inherited remnant in these beings. With
> the longing [the unfulfilled desire for a connection with higher
> beings that is no longer possible] we see egotism flare up at first
> in the weakest form, but then, with time, we see it quietly slip
> into the evolution of the world. And so we see how beings who
> have the longing to offer themselves, i.e., their egohood, are
> in certain respects, condemned to one-sidedness, to a life lived
> only in themselves unless something else enters in.

There are two motifs we should retain from this description: on the
one hand, a gentle *opposition*, an initial egohood stirs in the deferred
beings, that will then intensify; on the other hand, there is an unful-
filled *longing* in these beings for their lost connection to other beings,
which would be like a damnation if not ameliorated.

With these descriptions we can see, from within, so to speak, the
origin of the adversary powers. Their generation lies in the deeds and
abstention of the highest angelic beings. From their actions and renun-
ciation something comes forth that, at first gently, then increasingly
clearly, becomes the power of independence and adversity in evil.

The hindered beings are filled with a deep longing for their original
being. This longing must have led them to terrible desolation and loneliness. To balance this, beings from the second hierarchy brought them
something that did not eliminate the isolation but made it bearable. The
spirits of movement (Dynameis) came to these retarded beings thereby
setting them in motion, stimulating them and helping them overcome
their inner desolation.

> The experiences of these beings are powerfully intensified,
> in the way that would be the case with a human being who is
> constantly moving and thereby experiences and learns a great
> deal. This movement is translated into pictures within the
> deferred beings, pictures in which all that exists in the world is
> mirrored in various ways; a rich picture-consciousness results

from the inner and outer movement of these beings who are otherwise consumed with longing ... through the activity of the spirits of movement their inner being, which was otherwise empty, is filled, the inner being that suffers from longing is filled with a balsam that is poured into these beings in the form of pictures. Otherwise these beings would be empty in their souls, lacking in any kind of otherness that could not be called longing. But the balsam of pictures trickles in and fills the desolate emptiness with variety and in this way lead these beings through banishment and condemnation.

Death as the consequence

What began as a gentle egohood and opposition was powerfully intensified in the long course of evolution. For we are dealing with beings with great creative power, who, like other members of the highest hierarchy, were capable of shaping major portions of creation. Of course, in the further course of evolution beings from the lower realms of angels joined the ranks of these deferred angels — in that they were swept along in this entire development. These lower angels did not have the rank nor the creative power of the higher beings yet they joined them and together they created a new realm of existence. Powerful forces lived in the impeded beings, whom Rudolf Steiner therefore calls 'Beings with suppressed will.'

Normally this will would have flowed into the progression of creation, but this was no longer possible. The isolation of these beings caused them to circle with their own forces within themselves. Thrown back on themselves, trapped as it were within themselves, they could only achieve a monstrous degree of selfishness (especially the Luciferic beings), an egotism driven to extremes and an over-exaggerated feeling for self-worth.

On the other hand, the Ahrimanic beings, who had been rejected at an earlier stage than the Luciferic beings and, therefore, had a longer period of isolation behind them, were more equipped with forces for shaping the world (Lucifer predominantly rules the *forces in the soul*). Therefore, the Ahrimanic beings contributed not only to an intensification of egotism, but also to a condensation, hardening, rigidity, and even a kind of 'crampedness' of all being. The powerful forces and substance of Ahrimanic beings that otherwise would have gone freely into external creation is now — through the fact that it must be taken back into itself — drawn into itself; it hardens, rigidifies and dies. In denseness and heaviness, in the descent into death, which is the result of material existence, we see the consequences of the development taken by Ahriman.

When we consider *the will aspect* of the Adversaries, we see in Lucifer egotism multiplied into the unimaginable, and in the Ahrimanic powers we see condensation, hardening, sclerosis, rigidity up to and including the power to destroy resulting ultimately in the death of all being.

In this light we can also consider the consciousness of the beings that remained behind. How does their consciousness develop further? Excluded as it is from meaning and decisions of divine wisdom it must necessarily darken. The Adversaries no longer have access to the goals and meaning that are developed in the progression of creation; they can no longer 'understand' the decisions made by God; advancing creation is a riddle to them; they strive towards goals that are no longer a part of healthy evolution.

All this had an especially strong impact on the creation of man. The Adversaries could no longer understand why human beings had been created. They could not grasp the secret of creation, the strangest and least comprehensible being of all creation. They therefore turned all the power at their disposal against this being, and thus became Adversaries of God.

As the adversarial consciousness gradually darkened, the previously characterized *world of pictures* entered their consciousness. With this Luciferic beings carried within themselves not only all the colour and diversity of creation, but they also permeated these pictures with their power to create and form. They transformed these pictures into a world of images that worked in a free and independent fashion. Ingenious fantasy but also illusions became the content of Luciferic consciousness.

Because this kind of consciousness lives in Luciferic beings, they can become the inspiration for artistic activity that works freely using worldly images and forms. This is where they reveal their positive side. However, misleading fantasy and illusions are the shadow side of this kind of consciousness.

If Lucifer's consciousness of certain worldly realms is dimmed through illusory pictures, then the consciousness of Ahriman is completely darkened. In Ahriman's being, which carries within itself the forces of hardening and solidification, even the world of living pictures that is open to him must die. In his being they must lose their colour and movement, their inner glow and power, and degenerate into shadow and schematics.

As in art we find a mirror for Luciferic consciousness, so we find a reflection of Ahrimanic consciousness in the majestic world of technology and geometry. There is a world of pictures living here also; images that are fascinating and awe-inspiring. Their significance for the world is obvious, but all life is banned from it. In the hardening and rigidity of the will and the darkening of consciousness a 'will to oppose' had to ultimately arise in the Ahrimanic beings. A deep enmity against good, a will to do evil and bring death arose, a will directed above all against man and all that is human.

Death and destruction are the end points of a long development and are the pinnacle of evil. With them immense opposition to the will of God both in the world and in man, has come into being. Not just the *appearance* of evil but *real* evil has entered into existence.

The question of meaning

Consequently, the question arises: why did all this happen? Does it all have a meaning? Does that which we must call a sacrifice of the affected beings have meaning? This question of 'why' is connected to the fundamental question of human beings. What is man?

It is not easy today to consider this question; it seems misplaced and therefore eludes our understanding. From the scientific point of view man is seen in a certain light — as 'the naked ape' (with this term the current neo-Darwinian theory of evolution is not entirely mislabelled); as 'programmed man' and 'a dressed ape' (sociology and behaviourism). If these are ultimate truths concerning our humanity then there is nothing more to expect from us; then the claim that there is something connecting humans to a higher spiritual world, or that we somehow carry an image of God within us, is nothing more than illusion.

From the above characterizations we see that the true nature of man cannot be perceived without bringing the supersensible into consideration. Then we realize that what many suspect is true: our present-day picture of what the human being actually is represents only a partial reality, if it is true at all. John the Evangelist knew that there must be more to man and expressed this through his visionary powers: 'It does not yet appear, what we shall be.' (1John 3:2 RSV)

Today only a part of us has been revealed, even less than a fragment of our human essence. From this fragment the actual human being will develop in the future. From the part of our nature that has already developed we can 'read' how much God has already invested in us. The human body alone despite its frailties, which are derived from the work of the Adversaries, is a never-ending work of art; every individual organ is an astonishing world in itself. The way the organs harmonize and co-ordinate their work to constitute a 'body' can hardly be comprehended. In this lies a divine 'investment' of wisdom, substance and power that speaks of the greatness intended for mankind. This investment would be without meaning if it did not intend to equip humans for their destined vocation in a purely bodily nature.

We can see a reflection of these forces in the accomplishments of truly great people in the fields of art and science, as well as in the realm of self-sacrifice and self-discipline. The powers these people show us, which go beyond what is possible today, reveal the true measure of man. From this point of view it is not surprising that not only John but also Paul speaks in the New Testament of the mystery of a great human future. Paul even makes it clear that as long as man has not reached his measure and fulfilled the possibilities of his being, something must remain unredeemed in creation. In Romans 8:19, he says: 'For creation waits with eager longing for the revelation of the sons of God ...' The term 'sons of God' refers to *human beings*. Hidden in humanity, and yet to be revealed, is something through which other beings of creation will find their fulfilment and salvation.

Rudolf Steiner confirms this perspective of the human being. It is only the higher forces in us that are still unrevealed; he spoke of higher *soul-forces*, of intensified *life-forces*, and of the absolute control we will have over the earthly body in the future and over everything in material existence that shows itself today only from its Ahrimanic, external, side. The account of creation given at the beginning of the Bible, states not only that man is created in the image and likeness of God (Gen.1:26–28), but it further describes how God entrusts to Adam the naming of all creatures (Gen.2:19–21). The significance of the human being for creation in his relationship to God is expressed in both of these statements.

We have in nature a picture or parable for the undeveloped quality of man and his future possibilities. No one would suspect that a butterfly could emerge from a caterpillar. There is no sign of a 'higher destination or calling' — except perhaps for the wonderful colour found on many caterpillars — to be discovered in the earth-bound appearance of the caterpillar. And yet the butterfly must somehow be hidden in it, otherwise the butterfly could never emerge. We can learn to understand our current human condition in such a natural picture. What we see today in human beings is only a questionable fragment, but we carry within us hidden possibilities for the future.

Can we better grasp what these future possibilities are? What is the significance, the idea of man, of the human? An important hint lies in the ancient idea that man is a microcosm within the macrocosm, the larger world. That is, man is a summation of the great world in the small. The world, the cosmos, is an unlimited, abundant multiplicity, whose parts have been separated from one another. Every being, even the angels, carry some of this multiplicity within them, but only as a part of the whole. When the Godhead poured his being out into creation, every part of creation participated in its way — as part of the whole although in an individual way.

On the way to further development, however, the whole should be gathered together again. A being should arise that can realize not just a part, but the whole of the great world in a small world as if in a central location, the heart of the world. This being should be able to carry something of the best of all beings in itself. *Man is to be formed as the heart of the world.*

This explains the words 'image and likeness of God' for God also comprehends and includes everything. But God has poured himself into the multiplicity and abundance of all beings (but without being 'dissolved' into the world in the pantheistic sense.) This multiplicity and abundance is to be gathered together again and — after this mighty unfolding process — renewed in order to raise all of creation to a higher level. Man and mankind are not the insignificant beings in the universe that they might appear to be at first glance.

Christ is pointing to the future goal of human beings when, using an expression from the Old Testament (Ps.82:6), he says, 'You are gods' (John 10:34).

If we keep this in mind then the path to this goal acquires inner greatness. The caterpillar achieves its butterfly form only through a complete transformation of its bodily substance. The entire process of world evolution, including the development of evil, is required to extract this future form out of man and stimulate it into creative activity. We cannot overestimate the enormous significance of this process.

This lends a new perspective on Christ's behaviour when confronted by evil: He takes Judas into the circle of his disciples and accepts the betrayal that leads to his sacrificial death; he does not condemn the adulteress; Christ accepts the criminal crucified on the cross to his left into his kingdom. Much more could be mentioned. There is no clearer way to show that evil is an element in the world which must be recognized as serving good.

Of course we must not overlook how powerfully Christ steps forward against the working of evil: at the temptation, with the cleansing of the temple, when he corrects Peter at Caesarea Philippi ('Get behind me Satan!' Mark 8:33). The inclusion and transformation of evil are visible in Christ's attitude towards it, which is not merely rejection and opposition.

Man's creation in the 'image and likeness' of God also means human beings are intended to be inwardly free and creative. In order to call forth these qualities, a 'free space' had to be created in the universe, in which the divine is not active, in which it can even be denied and suppressed.

Freedom would not have been possible in close proximity to God, in 'paradise;' human beings would have lived in attraction to the divine, would have had to remain in childlike devotion and self-forgetting. The expulsion from paradise would not have happened. Humanity was therefore set free, and increasingly left to itself. This too is progress. Freedom means more than being free from eternal compulsion. Above all it means being able to completely take hold of oneself. This is an act that no one, not even God, can do for another person.

Summary

In the beginning there was the world of God that permeated all being and encompassed all beings. In that world the angelic beings of the hierarchies, lived in harmony with the divine. Everything was permeated by the essence and being of good because there was no contradiction anywhere. Everything was unfolded in mutually creative relationships.

However, with the world in this condition freedom did not arise, for it would have presupposed a rebellion of some kind. As long as the divine was present everywhere, permeating everything and everyone, no being could or wanted to set itself in opposition to God. The blessedness of being connected to God, the fascination with the majesty and power of divine existence was simply too great.

But man was destined for freedom. The possibility of turning against God and living without him had to be given to human beings. A theatre of action had to be created in the world, in which God's activity was not immediately present. Furthermore, beings had to be active there, who could push the human being away from God so that the highest powers for good would be called forth. It was not possible simply to create man in an already-free state. For freedom is an inner quality, an inner 'taking hold of oneself' and 'developing oneself.'

Deep down we should thank ourselves for our freedom, but it still needs to be called forth by evil. At the same time, in our encounter with evil, we receive the possibility of experiencing good not just as an echo of God's goodness but as something created in a completely free way out of ourselves and then set to work against evil. Creative action in freedom creates good. In order to equip human beings to do this to the highest degree the challenge also has to be of the highest degree. Elevated beings became bearers of intense evil but they are not simply playing an apparently evil role; they really are evil.

Since beings in close proximity to God cannot be evil, the first step towards evil was for God to separate hierarchal beings from himself, beings that were to become the Adversaries of man. However, this task was also a great sacrifice.

The descent took place over eons. Exclusion from the divine meant that the forces in these beings intensified within them and led to twisted distortions of their original intentions. In addition to this, their consciousness was darkened. Cut off from any understanding of the divine plan for salvation, these beings were no longer in a position to see and understand the great plan for world evolution, and the nature of their task in developing humanity.

Ultimately this development led to the creation of a mighty will opposing the divine. Evil arises when beings see their own powerful creative forces and spiritual might rejected by the progressive beings of the world, during eons of alienation from God. It arises when they find themselves excluded from the understanding and working of God, yet it cannot simply cease to be active. Spiritual forces unfold but are then limited to circling within, creating their own world of increasingly dark abysses, or a world of intensified false, yet brightly shining, light.

The Adversaries gained access to that region of the world intended for humanity; this theatre of action, where human lives and history unfold far from God, and where we are called to discover the meaning of life. The Adversaries and mankind meet on earth and the mighty forces, at the disposal of the Adversaries, are introduced to humanity. All of this has resulted in the present-day condition of the world.

Evil then has come into existence for the sake of man. Above all, it is active on earth and in humanity. Does this perhaps signify that we will one day have a special responsibility to guide the powers of evil back into the whole, to unite them again with God in harmony with the hierarchies?

Expressed in the language of fairy tales: if evil is the result of an enchantment, then who will break the spell? If evil (the devil) has a daughter, who unites with good, what kind of future can the daughter expect? Must she always remain connected with evil?

Part Two

The Adversaries in the Human Being

CHAPTER 6

Suffering and Guilt

Our look at fairy tales has already led us to consider questions of destiny. The ethic of the path, powers of transformation available in danger and suffering, and the motif of redemption can be seen as factors that give life meaning. With this in mind, we turn to one concrete destiny in particular.

When considering the experience of evil there is one figure that stands out among the many personalities who have struggled with destiny in ancient and even modern times. In his life and destiny Job demonstrates the suffering that plays a role in every human life.

Job — suffering without guilt

The story of Job is one of the most magnificent and gripping in the Old Testament. Through the centuries it has repeatedly held people spellbound. Job is beset by great suffering and trials, yet he is guilty of nothing. In every regard he is a noble, upstanding, righteous and pious man. He was 'God fearing and avoided evil' according to the story. God himself testifies to Job's innocence and adds 'there is no one like him in all the land' (Job 2:8).

We are dealing here with someone who is an outstanding personality and who has incurred no guilt whatsoever, and yet God allows him to be beset by every imaginable misfortune. After God gives Satan power over him, Job is torn away from his wealth and comfort in a single day and thrown into poverty and loneliness. Messengers announce to him the destruction of his herds and fields by enemy hordes and the death of all his children through misfortune. He is left behind, alone with his wife. At the end of the first chapter we read: 'Job stood up and tore his clothes and pulled his hair and fell on the earth and prayed and spoke: Naked I came into the world, naked I will leave it. The Lord gives and the Lord takes away; blessed be the name of the Lord. In all of this Job did not sin and he said nothing foolish against God.' Even after all that Job is able to preserve his piety.

In the second chapter his suffering is increased. Job is afflicted by terrible diseases. His body is covered with 'angry' boils from the soles of his feet to the top of his head. We read: 'And he took a shard and scraped himself and sat in the ashes. And his wife spoke to him. Are you clinging to your righteousness? Curse God and die! But he spoke to her. You speak as the foolish women speak. Have we not received good from God and should we not also take evil from him? In all of this, Job did not sin with his lips.'

The book of Job is concerned with the question of innocent suffering. The question is sharply posed in a situation so extreme that it is unlikely any mortal would ever have to face it. Furthermore, Job really is without guilt. The reader cannot avoid the problem that here truly terrible calamities befall an innocent man. Why? Is there any meaning to it?

In the literature I am familiar with there is no real answer. Many writers have said that Job offers a special example of piety, a man of extraordinary patience, who shows us that even in meaningless suffering the higher wisdom and goodness of God must be acknowledged. Yet this cannot be the true intention of the story. A meaning like this could never justify the horrors that God makes Job experience. A God whose actions stemmed from such intentions would himself be highly questionable.

Another way of explaining Job is to find in him a hidden arrogance, which can be heard in his words (provoked by his suffering), and ultimately he is humbled. In this case Job is, after all, a sinner who is trying to justify himself before God and finally, in the face of God's overwhelming omnipotence and wisdom, must throw himself into the dust. But it seems to me that this is an untenable exegesis because Job has been declared to be 'without sin.' This too would present us with a God unworthy of devotion, a God who likes to see people crawling in the dust like worms.

God and Satan

None less than C.G. Jung (1875–1961) suggested a third way to explain the riddle. In his book, *The Answer to Job*, he attempts to explain in an ingenious fashion that the problem actually lies in the Old Testament God, Yahweh, himself. Yahweh has not only a good side, but also an evil side, which is personified in Satan and, so to speak, shoved aside, but for this very reason has not been mastered. Job becomes a sacrifice to the evil stirrings of Yahweh. He opposes these stirrings but without success. For Yahweh would not be himself if he could admit that he acted evilly and unjustly against Job. For this reason, in the end, Yahweh can only crush Job.

Jung writes:

> Yahweh projects onto Job a sceptic's face which he does not
> like because it is his own, and which gazes at him with an
> uncanny and critical eye. He is afraid of it, for only when
> faced with something frightening does one mobilize a list of
> references to one's power, cleverness, courage, invincibility,
> etc. ... Yahweh's speeches have the unthinking, yet none the
> less transparent, purpose of showing Job the brutal power of
> the demiurge: 'This is I, the creator of all the ungovernable,
> ruthless forces of nature, which are not subject to any ethical
> laws. I, too, am an amoral force of nature, a purely phenomenal
> personality that cannot see its own back.'[1]

This 'back' that Yahweh does not 'see' is his dark, demonic side; it is, according to Jung, Satan. He 'projects' this side of his unconscious being onto Job and crushes him for this reason. Job is then, an innocent sacrifice to the evil side of God, to whom he is helplessly exposed.

Of all the various attempts at answering the riddle of Job, Jung's is certainly the most interesting. But is it sufficient? It also starts with the assumption that Job is crushed in the end, when exactly the opposite is the case. Jung's understanding of the relationship between God and Satan is excessively psychologized. What lives as soul stirrings in human beings becomes a being or beings in the spiritual world. There really are beings striving against beings. We have already seen in the last chapter that, in the end, Satan must have originated in the all encompassing being of God.

Behind the question of innocent suffering stands the relationship between good and evil, between God and Satan. This question is also sharply posed in the Book of Job. In our discussion of the angelic realms we have already seen that, amazingly enough, Satan appears among the angels, also in the Book of Job. 'Now there came the day when the Sons of God came to present themselves before the Lord, and Satan also came among them. The Lord said to Satan, "Where have you come?" Satan answers the Lord, "From going to and fro on the earth, and from walking up and down on it".' (Job 1:6f).

And then the Lord does something that is truly hard to grasp: he draws Satan's attention to Job. 'And the Lord said to Satan, Have you considered my servant, Job, that there is none like him on the earth, a blameless and upright man, who fears God and turns away from evil?' (1:8). God is actually provoking Satan. Does he not know what he is calling forth? We find the same situation in Goethe's *Faust*: God draws the attention of Mephistopheles to Faust. There are only two ways to understand this: either 'divine' carelessness, not to say punishable naiveté or ignorance, is at work here — or a higher intention.

Satan immediately makes use of the opportunity and interprets Job's piety in his own way. 'Then Satan answered the Lord, "Does Job fear God for naught? Hast thou not put a hedge about him and his house and all that he has on every side? Thou hast blessed the work of his hands, and his possessions have increased in the land. But put forth thy hand now and touch all that he has, and he will curse thee to thy face' (1:9–11). And now events take their fatal course. Satan receives express permission from God to shower Job with misfortune. 'And the Lord said to Satan, "Behold all that he has is in your power; only upon himself do not put forth your hand".' (1:12). We know what then happens: with God allowing it, Satan brings Job to the edge of his existence.

In Chapter 2, Satan appears again, the conversation is repeated and now Satan has permission to attack Job's physical well-being. How can God allow this? Even provoke it? Is there an intention and meaning behind it all?

Job's elevation

The Book of Job has forty-two chapters. Chapters 4 to 37 are filled with the speeches of Job's four friends, primarily concerning Job's struggle to understand the meaning of his destiny (twenty chapters). One must read the text very carefully in order to follow the steps taken in this struggle. The translation of the Book of Job presents special difficulties because it contains an ancient, in many instances difficult to understand, Hebrew. There are probably also gaps in the text that has been handed down to us.

At first it appears as though Job's complaint is repeated constantly for twenty chapters and expresses essentially the same thing in different words: 'God has smite me but I am innocent.' But a closer inspection shows that in three places the text indicates the progress that Job has made in his suffering.

The first we find in the tenth chapter: 'I will say to God, do not condemn me; let me know why thou dost contend against me. Does it seem good to thee to oppress, to despise the work of thy hands? ... If I sin, thou dost mark me, and dost not acquit me of my iniquity' (10:2f&14).

Job is asking why God is so engaged in his suffering, why he doesn't simply extinguish him if Job is so reprehensible to him. A first dawning of God's intention shines in this question. The second location is in the sixteenth chapter. The speeches of his friends that may seem endless to us are not without their results. Job rises to a further insight: 'O earth, cover not my blood, and let my cry find no resting place. Even now, behold my witness is in heaven, and he that vouches for me is on high. My friends scorn me; my eye pours out tears to God, that he would maintain the right of a man with God, like that of a man with his neighbour' (16:18–21).

In the tenth chapter the question arose in Job as to *why* God was so concerned with him, whether his suffering really was so significant. Here he realizes that his suffering reaches up to heaven, that he has there someone who vouches for him who is involved in his human situation. This was an extremely unusual idea. Through his suffering, Job is brought close to an understanding of Christ. That this is the case is shown us by the famous nineteenth chapter: 'Oh that my words were written! Oh that they were inscribed in a book! Oh that with an iron pen and lead they were graven in the rock forever! For I know that my Redeemer lives, and at last he will stand up on the earth; and after my skin has been thus destroyed, then from my flesh I shall see God.' (19:23–26).

Rudolf Steiner has pointed out this passage in Job and confirmed that it reveals a preliminary awareness of the Resurrection Body (the human body in *spiritualized* form. 'I know that my Redeemer lives.' These words have become very well known, in part because of Handel's *Messiah*.

Job consciously struggles from step to step increasing his understanding. Job's experience is intensified until he has reached the point
where he can turn directly to God and challenge him to answer. And
God answers him, which is by itself something extraordinary. This
answer from God is connected with another step for Job.

The vision of God

Job's attainment of a vision of God is one of the most striking events
in the Old Testament. Because of its importance, we must be very clear
about why it is so extraordinary.

There is an old saying, 'He who sees God, dies.' This means that
mortals cannot bear the sight of God. The fact that human beings do
not see God and can therefore deny even the existence of God is connected not only with the spiritual blindness of man, but above all with
the fact that the power of God's proximity must destroy man. Angelus
Silesius expresses this with the words: 'God dwells in a light, to which
the path is barred. Who does not become it, he will never see him.'
This is also an indication of a *path* to approaching divine being. John's
Gospel speaks the same way: 'No one has ever seen God with his eyes;
the only born son, who was within the Father has become the leader in
this vision (John 1:18 JM).

This points to the fact that proximity to God is, to begin with, inaccessible to human beings because they could not bear it. The picture
language of the story of the Fall from paradise speaks of a Cherub
standing at the gate to paradise blocking entrance with a 'flaming
sword.' Job, however, breaks through to a vision of God. Through
his struggle and suffering he acquires the strength to call to God in
such a way that God answers him directly. Furthermore, Job is able to
endure the answer and the presence of God without perishing before
the power of God. He can say, 'Until now I have only heard of you
with my ears but now my eye has seen you.' Through suffering something has arisen in Job that was not there before; his piety was only
traditional, he had only heard of God 'with is ears.' But now he has
acquired the power of sight that allows him to enter the immediate
presence of God.

Job thereby stands as one of the outstanding figures in the Old
Testament. What can only be said in the great moments, in the excep-
tional situations in the Old Testament, can now be said of Job: He

has seen God and survived the moment. The fruit of his suffering is a higher relationship to God.

Of course, he bows in deepest humility before the vision of God but he is not destroyed. On the contrary, the progression of events shows that his attitude before God is recognized while the attitude of his friends, who were constantly trying to find guilt in his behaviour, is reprimanded.

> After the Lord has spoken these words to Job, the Lord said to Eliphaz the Temanite: 'My wrath is kindled against you and against your two friends; for you have not spoke of me what is right, as my servant Job has. Now therefore take seven bulls and seven rams, and go to my servant Job, and offer up for yourselves a burnt offering; and my servant Job shall pray for you, for I will accept his prayer not to deal with you according to your folly; for you have not spoken of me what is right, as my servant Job has.' So Eliphaz the Temanite and Bildad the Shuhite and Zophar the Naamathite went and did what the Lord had told them; and the Lord accepted Job's prayer. And the Lord restored the fortunes of Job, when he had prayed for his friends; and the Lord gave Job twice as much as he had before. (42:7–10).

Since Job is elevated by the suffering that leads to his vision of God, a new perspective is possible on the words of judgment God speaks to him in Chapters 38 to 41. God's answer to Job, which was provoked by Job's outcry, begins:

> Then the Lord answered Job out of the whirlwind: 'Who is this that darkens counsel by words without knowledge? Gird up your loins like a man, I will question you and you will answer me. Where were you when I laid the foundation of the earth? Tell me if you have understanding' (38:2–4).

These words of God have been misinterpreted in many ways. They have been understood as punishment or chastisement and could easily appear that way. They consist of a majestic reminder of the creative deeds of God. It would be easy to conclude that God, with this reminder of his omnipotence, wanted to bring an end to Job's reprimanding criticism of God's action. This misinterpretation is understandable. However, a closer look shows it to be both trivial and unjustified. Several decisive sentences that provide a key to understanding what is actually going on have been consistently overlooked.

'Where were you when I laid the foundation of the earth? Tell me if you have understanding.' Of course there is no possibility of Job giving an answer to this question. Apparently he is supposed to be crushed. But then a number of such questions are linked in sequence, which ultimately lead to these words:

'Have you entered into the springs of the sea, or walked in the recesses of the deep? Have the gates of death been revealed to you, or have you seen the gates of deep darkness? Have you comprehended the expanse of the earth? Declare, if you know all this' (38:16–18). And then comes the big surprise when the text continues: 'You know, for you were born then, and the number of your days is great!' (38:21).

'For you were born then,' belongs to the question, 'Where were you when I laid the foundation of the earth?' This can only mean 'You were present at creation.' God is pointing out man's connection to the original creation and man's deeply hidden knowledge or understanding of the mysteries of creation. 'You know ...' Of course, Job must admit that in his present knowledge he is aware of nothing of all this. But God's answer, within the composition of the Book of Job, can have only been meaningful if it represents a first dawning in Job to the mysteries of the world born out of pain and suffering. God's words are intended to lead Job to take hold of his higher self, which lives united with the mysteries of creation.

This can remind us of Jacob Boehme's response to the question, 'How can you write about the secrets of creation, paradise, the original state of Adam etc?' He said, 'Why are you surprised? I was there!'

As pre-earthly human beings united with God, we were present at creation. God's words to Job remind us of this fact. One could misinterpret these words and understand them as ironic, mocking comments from the mouth of God. Yet what kind of God would that be who uses derision and irony in the face of human suffering?

God did not want to crush and mock Job. All of this makes sense if we consider together these three facts.
1. God himself points Job out to Satan.
2. Job comes to a vision of God — rare in the Old Testament.
3. Job is justified before his friends when God expressly says: 'Job spoke rightly.'

God's intention could only have been to elevate Job; and this could only happen through suffering, brought on by Satan's 'help.' The fruit of this suffering is Job's vision of God and his consciousness approaching that knowledge hidden to earthly consciousness yet available to the 'higher self.' That is, the knowledge that we were present at creation, that our true being is eternal. This consciousness is called forth or provoked by God's words to him. He breaks through to a vision of God out of this consciousness. This is the only explanation that gives the Book of Job meaning.

God's concluding speech shows this to be the case. After the mysteries of creation are pointed out to Job the twofold nature of the Adversaries is shown to him. This is the conclusion and high point of God's address. 'Behemoth' and 'Leviathan' are explained to Job. He becomes privy to the knowledge that God has included the Adversaries in his plan for creation and at the same time holds them within limits. One of the greatest descriptions of Lucifer and Ahriman to be found anywhere in world literature is presented here in the Old Testament.

Concerning Behemoth/Ahriman we read: 'He is the first of the works of God ...' Job is to understand that evil belongs to creation and were co-creators of the cosmos, the greatness of which is revealed to him in the Lord's speech. For then he can understand how evil is to contribute to the progress of man's creation, how his suffering becomes the thorn that pushes him to grow closer to God. We see how for Job a vision of the Adversaries becomes a path to the vision of God. For only after the vision of Behemoth and Leviathan does Job say, 'Now my eye sees thee.'

A mighty picture stands before us at the end of the Book of Job. Lucifer and Ahriman in the depths, and above them the Godhead himself who holds the Adversaries within bounds. This picture reminds us of what Rudolf Steiner portrayed in his sculpture, 'The Representative of Man,' which portrays Lucifer and Ahriman with Christ holding them in check.

Job was able to take an extraordinary step in inner development through his suffering. Apparently, Satan did not know this; his consciousness was darkened to the point where he could not see ahead to what would happen. He had to serve as a tool of a higher purpose that was able to lead Job to an intensification and elevation of his being through an overwhelming challenge. Perhaps here lies the meaning of all suffering.

One last remark about Job's destiny. In the Old Testament, Job, the innocent sufferer, appears to prefigure Christ's innocent suffering. Christ was also handed over to evil even though he was innocent. Also, from this suffering a great good came forth, but for all mankind. The Book of Job contains elements that point to Christ. Hence, Job can be called a forerunner or 'model' of Christ, but the reverse is also true. Christ fulfils the destiny of Job. He perfects it and, at the same time, makes it into an archetype for every human being who struggles with his destiny.

CHAPTER 7

Evil in Human Beings

The evil that comes from individual human beings, from their intentions and weaknesses, from their personal depravity and passions, from their stupidity or excessive zeal could be called 'everyday evil.' This is the realm where personal guilt and responsibility appear. The figure of Faust, as Goethe paints him, portrays many of these motifs in an archetypal fashion. From him we can gain an impression of how, in this realm, meaning, healing, and redemption are also possible.

The human soul served as a gate of entry for the first distortions of human nature and for the working of Lucifer. Lucifer gave man the impulse towards freedom and stirred up the ability to acquire knowledge independently; but at the same time he caused egotism to flare up into the soul.

Egotism: the intervention of Lucifer

According to Rudolf Steiner there are two forces that underlie all stirrings in the human soul: the power of sympathy and the power of antipathy: 'The force with which one soul-form attracts others, seeks to melt together with them, to put forward and stress its kinship with them, must be designated as *sympathy. Antipathy*, on the other hand, is the force with which soul-forms repel, exclude one another in the soul-world with which they assert *their separate, unique identity*'[1] (last italics from HWS). We are not using the usual meanings of sympathy and antipathy here, but using these words to designate the fundamental forces in the soul, the forces that determine all kinds of human feelings.

We find the power of sympathy in its purest form in a small child. Without reservation, the small child turns to its surroundings open and full of trust, ready to receive what comes. Also with a child we can see how this openness to the world soon changes. Slowly but surely egotism awakens in the soul. If the child is not properly educated this growing egotism can escalate to the point where he or she becomes an unbearable tyrant. We can observe here the powerful awakening of antipathy, the soul force in human beings that enables them not only to flow out into the world in devotion, but also forces them to come to themselves.

The child's experience of the world is that of being entirely melted together with it. A small child is not yet able to distinguish between inner and outer worlds. The antipathetic element, that 'asserts their separate, unique identity' — as Rudolf Steiner wrote — has not yet taken hold of the child. Sympathy in very early childhood, when no antipathy has yet appeared, leads the child to experience him- or herself at one with all being. The human soul in paradise was similar: fully devoted to the divine and flowing together with the spiritual world.

It is certainly clear that antipathy must assert itself for the human being to pull together. This begins in the moment when the external world 'appears' to the child's perception as a separate experience; in this moment the child's separate identity, their experience of selfhood, begins. We have here the effects of Lucifer's work in human biography tangibly before us.

In the biography of humanity it was the moment of the Fall into sin that brought about a similar change in the soul of mankind. Lucifer caused the power of self-aggrandizement and self-will that lived in his own being to 'flow into' the human soul, which was still primarily sympathy-filled and, therefore, wide open to external influences. With this event mankind began to distance itself from its surroundings and to feel its own unique selfhood. This distancing from God with the help of the serpent is vividly described in the Bible.

The snake's clever question displays a first step away from God: 'Did God say, "You shall not eat of any tree of the garden?"' Doubt is gently injected into the human soul. It is a seed for the first step back from God, a first impulse of antipathy. The antipathetic gesture comes towards us even more powerfully in the next words when the snake gives a direct denial of God's word to Adam and Eve. 'You will not die.' Denial is a pure linguistic expression of antipathy. We see the snake's words of doubt — the seed of antipathy — grow and blossom into denial, a full expression of antipathy.

What then follows is a full escalation. God is not only doubted and denied, but dishonourable motives for the command are imputed to him. The accusation of acting out of egotism is suddenly directed at God himself; what the serpent has in himself — egotism — is projected onto God with the following words: 'For God knows that when you eat of it your eyes will be opened, and you will be like God, knowing good and evil' (Gen.3:5).

Step by step we can follow the 'stepping-back' manoeuvres set in place for Adam and Eve by the snake: first there is doubt, then denial of what God said, finally suspicion that God has an impure, egotistical motive. In just a few steps we see the power of antipathy proliferate with eerie might. Adam and Even have nothing with which to oppose the manoeuvres of the snake. They absorb the snake's influence with full sympathy. To oppose this influence they would need the power of antipathy, which is only just beginning to arise in them because of the snake.

The final intensification of the snake's insinuations comes with the words that remind us of the promised 'image and likeness of God' and therefore call up a deep longing: '... you will be like God.' With these words the snake finally achieves its goal. The movement back from God, created in Adam and Eve through the snake's words, now has a positive content.

The reminder that man was created in the image and likeness of God stimulates desire and egotism. With this achieved we have arrived at the full effects of Lucifer's work. For sympathy and antipathy are completely mixed in desire. Pure antipathy would not desire but reject; pure sympathy would devote itself to something other than itself but not be able to desire anything for itself. Antipathy is found in desiring in 'for me' — and not for another. Sympathy is at work in the desire to take hold of something, to reach out. Lucifer not only stimulates the gesture of antipathy in the soul, but he also — and this is characteristic of Lucifer — mixes it strongly with sympathy. This mixture causes desire to well up in the soul.

The Luciferic aspect of this process is seen further in the fact that it serves self-aggrandizement. All desire, all egotism in the end aims to intensify the experience of self, the experience of well-being. For this reason, we find in all desire the usually unconscious hidden ideal: 'you will be like God'.

The Fall into sin unites desire for the fruit with desire to become like God. Lucifer puts the ideal of becoming like God into the human soul in such a way that it seems as though it might be attainable through one simple deed. This is an illusion in light of the fact that, in reality, this ideal requires a long path of realization. All desire has a Luciferic illusion at its foundation — as if the pleasure found in fulfilling a desire could also contain the fulfilment of a deeper longing: the desire for an intensification of our power and our individual self. Self-intensification, also known as self-aggrandizement — and the underlying striving for 'God-likeness' under the sign of the snake — underlies all desire.

The human experience of self under the 'sign of the snake' has two characteristics: it appears as if happiness were easily attainable if only the soul's desire could be fulfilled and it appears as if happiness must always be sought in something forbidden and achieved 'against God.' The attractions of all that is 'forbidden' play a large role in desire. What is not forbidden is not desired. Desire accompanies the intensified assertion of self with the fullest expression of egotism.

The first of these two characteristics is an illusion that Lucifer is always able to awaken in human beings. I do not mean to speak against the joys of existence and the pleasures of life. On the contrary, those who are able to see through the illusions spoken of here, will be all the more able to rejoice at what life brings them. The second characteristic is a deeply rooted attitude towards life that is not easily overcome.

Through the Fall, the discovery of self is connected, from the beginning, with the rising up of egotism and desire, and their accompanying illusions. Thereby the doors of the soul are opened to various longings, instincts and passions, including the deepest stirrings of sensuality. They are all variations of desire, of the mixture of sympathy and antipathy. The influence of the snake begins to proliferate in this realm. The Fall into sin becomes fatal. Of course, the human ability *to know* was also developed by this process. Forming pictures and ideas in the mind, and the act of knowing itself, are also connected with antipathy. In a sense, any thought, notion or image in the human mind, must be separated from the human being having that thought, or beholding that image in their mind. The contents of human consciousness are *objects* beheld by the human *subject*. They have been distanced, separated from the human self, by the power of antipathy in order to be thought. Of course, sympathy is also involved for we must turn our attention to the contents of our thought.

Lucifer attained power over human beings through the Fall. Man thereby experienced egotism for the first time and simultaneously himself *as a self*. It is impossible now for human beings to get free of this experience of self. Lucifer's magic continues to work. 'The characteristic common to all evil is nothing other than egotism,' and 'fundamentally speaking all human evil proceeds from what we call egotism.'[2]

In a classical fashion, Albert Görres has characterized the roots of evil:

> Why is restless discontent so characteristic for man? Why can't he rest easily when he has what he needs? He is a bottle without a bottom, the more he has, the more he wants. Where does this excess of drive come from?
>
> Man is so insatiable because as a spiritual being he expects what we say to one another at every parting, *Alles Gute* [all good things] which means, 'I wish you all good things.'
>
> Man's need to have more being, more fullness of life, this universal desire to possess is the root of all unrest, of the heart, of the spirit and the senses.
>
> How much must man participate in being, how much does he want from life? The classical anthropological answer is: He wants it all. Man has what he needs and wants only when he can arrange to have the infinite being of God. He is not really at peace with bourgeois, home gardening. Boethius, the Chancellor for Theodoric, does not exaggerate when he says: What man needs to be happy is not all kinds of things but rather nothing less than the greatest thing: the certain possession of the total sum and perfection of the Good. The boundless hunger for being and the mind's limitless power to encompass is the foundation of all Good and the abyss of all evil.[3]

Man's striving to participate in the full being of the world, his 'boundless hunger for being' is his aim to become 'the image and likeness of God.' As Görres says in this striving to rise above himself lies not only 'the abyss of all evil' (perhaps we should limit this to 'an abyss'), but also the 'foundation of the Good;' namely when this power of striving is properly developed and directed towards the goal. Görres describes how far we can follow this striving in evil:

Evil makes one like a god. Ultimately every unjust deed offers a feeling of freedom, the sovereign independence from law and from the law giver, independence from the dictatorship of a hierarchy of values that we have not created ourselves, over which we wield no power unless we use the method of destructive leveling ...

I determine what my highest value is — this sentence feels fabulously godlike. The one who breaks the law is not only like God, he is superior to him, he can afford to do and enjoy what God forbids but cannot hinder.

We have now considered one of the roots of evil. It has always been more or less clearly seen in Christianity. Egotism, desire in all its forms then became in traditional Christianity actual sin; indeed, egotism is the *starting point* for all evil. But that is not all that connects the human soul with the Adversaries. In light of all that has been said about the duality of evil we know that Lucifer is not all of the story. How does Ahriman work in human souls?

Fear: the chains of Ahriman

Lucifer's intervention into the human soul draws in Ahriman. As a consequence of egotism, fear arises in the soul: a powerful force that appears in the soul like a shadow. Fear, anxiety and worry are the Ahrimanic consequences of egotism, of being cut off from the spiritual world. As long as the human being remained united with the spiritual world, he was carried and protected by higher beings. When he separated from it and lost his view into that world, he also lost the overview of his own path. The world became dark and Ahriman suddenly stands at his side stirring up fear, which is the other dark force (after egotism) that works deeply into the soul, with the effect that the door to the spiritual world is slammed shut with finality.

Anxiety, fear and worry are an *intensified* form of antipathy. While Lucifer predominantly uses sympathy with antipathy only employed as a secondary force to bring about a distancing, Ahriman's work is based, above all, on antipathy. Anxiety, fear and worry cause the soul to contract within itself and prevents it from turning to the world in an active and trusting way.

Let us remember how the Luciferic and Ahrimanic one-sided

extremes lined up in opposition to each other. On the 'Ahrimanic side' we find cowardice, greed, pedantry, paralysing inhibition, asceticism, cold heartedness, depression, etc.

The fear component is very clear in some of these characteristics, for instance in cowardice, greed (with simultaneous egotism), paralysing inhibition and depression. With others it is more hidden but also present, for instance the inability to go beyond oneself, to lose oneself in others. These are varieties of fear, for example, pedantry, cold heartedness and even the tendency towards abstraction in thinking, which is, of course, necessary and yet can serve as a defence against the concrete reality of life lived to the fullest. It is clear that the forces of antipathy have the upper hand in all of these soul qualities, whereas the opposite extremes — recklessness, wasteful extravagance, licentiousness — reveal a Luciferic intensification of self with sympathy predominant.

These one-sided extremes clearly display self-seeking (intensification of self) and fear (worry) as the effects of the two Adversaries in the soul, whereby we must remember that both extremes can be present at the same time. Greed displays both fear and egotism, with the fear side, the 'hanging onto oneself,' predominating, otherwise money or wealth would be spent to enhance the experience of pleasure. Hanging on to oneself is simultaneously experienced an egotistical intensification of self. Many soul gestures contain a polarity such as this. One adversary draws the other in after him; however, one of them always predominates.

Why fear appears in the human soul as the second manifestation of the Adversaries' power, and why it represents a final slamming shut of the door to the spiritual world, becomes clear in light of an additional fact. Fear is an intensification of egotism when antipathy is dominant. Someone succumbing to this emotion finds it impossible to draw near to the spiritual world; for approaching the spirit requires sympathy and the suppression of egotism.

Ahriman generates not only fear and anxiety, in general but, specifically, fear of the spiritual world. We begin to fear that we must surrender something of ourselves, that we must change if we are to stand before the spirit — and we do not want to do this. Therefore we avoid any approach to the spiritual world; we fear it.

This is the actual reason many people hold back from any serious involvement with spiritual striving. It is often entirely hidden or covered over by external busyness. Frequently, fear of the spirit is camouflaged as aggression against anything spiritual, or as hate, or as a declared lack of interest in anything spiritual. Following this thought, Görres says, 'Spiritual unwillingness and inactivity can take possession of the will ... usually under cover of involved and exhausting distractions. Someone who is deeply lethargic can appear to himself and others as diligent and very busy.'

Fear of death also contains some of this kind of fear. People often fear death because they instinctively feel how profound the transformation will be when they enter the spiritual world. They sense how much of what they egotistically strive to hang onto will have to be given up.

The biblical account of the Garden of Eden shows that fear must appear as a consequence of the Fall. It first appears as the fear of God. Adam and Eve hide themselves from God out of fear and shame. The expulsion from paradise is connected with this. The way Adam and Eve were constituted after the expulsion meant that they could no longer endure the presence of God.

Many psychologists say that the psychological problems of most people today are connected with far reaching conscious or unconscious fears, which often have no external cause at all. They work deeply in the soul as independent forces that cannot be mastered by any conscious effort.

> Fear, psychologically considered, is a torturing, objectless
> feeling of being threatened, always affecting one's entire
> existence, permeating and ruling it. It can appear without
> a specific location within, but also as a localized feeling
> (oppression of the heart or headache) and, especially with the
> mentally ill, it can intensify into severe disturbances of one's
> sense of well-being and personal being (fear neuroses). Fear
> is accompanied by physical symptoms: feeling of pressure,
> suffocation, claustrophobia, skipped heart beats, shock, etc. Fear
> is followed by these symptoms: dimming of consciousness,
> paralysation of the will, flight in senseless actions, reckless acts
> of violence against oneself and others.[4]

Precisely these last symptoms — feelings of pressure, suffocation, claustrophobia, etc. — depict very clearly the Ahrimanic character of fear. Görres continues: 'Overcoming fear is one of the greatest problems in practical psychotherapy because anxiety neuroses occurring in the most varied forms are among the most wide spread diseases of modern times.'

Görres, whose balanced approach and competence we are glad to make use of (though we do not agree with all the details), makes the following judgment of this fundamental problem:

> There are, to begin with, three hindrances that stand in the way of overcoming evil: The *fear* that we would miss out on the best that life has to offer and destroy our happiness if we leave off from evil. In psychoanalytic language this fear is called 'loss anxiety,' 'fear of separation.'
>
> The second hindrance is clinging to 'things' and persons that we consider as unsurrenderable conditions of our happiness (Freud and Jung would say: the libido): pleasure, sex, money, prestige, power, love from others, and a sense of belonging. Traditional language calls these the roots of evil: disordered dependence on finite values and on oneself. (These are also ordered dependencies!)
>
> We can summarize these roots of evil in two key concepts: fear of loss and self indulgence.

In Görres' two key concepts we see the characteristic motifs of Luciferic and Ahrimanic tendencies. Görres continues: 'The third hindrance is the lack of any motivation that could give illumination and energy,' i.e., a motivation towards good. This motif is also extremely important.

In our time we have seen an escalation of fear into despair, which also plays a big role in modern life. In people who find themselves in the terrible state of despair where the soul does 'not know which way to turn,' Ahriman truly has the upper hand. Later we will see that this condition of the soul is created, or at least fostered, by our present materialistically-orientated civilization.

In the final analysis, despair is the basis of every kind of evil in the soul. Görres says:

> Evil is despair. It always contains the feeling of resignation that one will have no luck with the good, that it is not possible to really be good and, therefore, it doesn't even pay even to start with it ... that means that the deepest longing in the human soul is discarded as an illusion.

We have here the other pole, the opposite extreme of immoderate striving towards self-aggrandizement, towards becoming like God. When we become aware of the inappropriateness, the unachievable aspect of this striving to be like God then this awareness itself again becomes an impulse towards evil: Lucifer and Ahriman are playing catch. The good lies in the middle, in a quiet striving for good, even if it at first appears to lie at an unattainable distance.

Worry is another relative of fear. Here we do not mean a justified 'caution' and making provisions for the future, but rather a withering, fruitless worry that fills us with fear, and yet is not able to change anything. These are worrisome thoughts that paint a frightful future yet are unable to contribute anything to master the future. They only weaken the soul and lead us astray. For usually the future turns out differently anyway from what our worries had led us to fear. In worry we devote our soul-forces to illusions. Just as Lucifer creates illusions through desire and self-aggrandizement, Ahriman conjures illusory pictures of fear and worry. Again we see clearly the work of the two Adversaries.

It is significant that until the seventeenth century fear as a consequence of the Fall did not play a role — as far as we know — in intellectual history. Of course in John's Gospel Christ, in his 'farewell address' (14–7), points to it when he says: 'In the world you have distress but take courage, I have overcome the world' (John 16:33). And worry is mentioned as a foe in the soul of the Gospels (Matt.6:25ff; Luke 21:34: a warning about egotism in eating and drinking and about worry). But it has only been since the Renaissance that fear has appeared as a problem in the theatre of theological and philosophical speculation. This fact is no doubt connected to the intensification of the Ahrimanic influence on mankind that began with the arrival of the Renaissance. Yet we can measure how little fear has been recognized as a religious and psychological factor by the fact that the word 'fear' has only appeared in German dictionaries of philosophy since 1950. This shows us how much desire as a sin has predominated. The motif of fear has become truly significant in the more recent philosophical movement called existentialism, especially in the work of Heidegger and Sartre. Of course, Kierkegaard was the first to treat the subject of fear extensively. With the discovery of fear has also come the surprise that it also has positive aspects. Is there perhaps a 'good' to be achieved by having to wrestle with Ahrimanic forces?

Egotism and fear are the terrible roots of evil in the human soul.

By speaking of 'roots' we are using a picture that contains within it an indication that there is an even deeper force, a 'ground for the roots,' of evil, in which egotism and fear are based.

Rudolf Steiner left no doubt that evil extends deeply into the being of man. He says that every human being has present within him an 'abyss of evil' that is connected with the previously described forces of antipathy, yet lies even deeper, hidden so to speak 'under the mirror of our memories.' According to Steiner this abyss reaches into our bodily constitution and is united there with the metabolic forces of destruction. These destructive forces are, of course, essential for human digestion (breaking down the foods we eat). This abyss is simultaneously connected to our soul and forms a foundation for our thinking activity and the activity of our 'I', our conscious self. It is best if one reads such ideas from spiritual science for oneself.[5]

The ideas presented above may seem less startling if one considers that the light and warmth of a candle flame exist only because a process that destroys matter is also present. It is well known how much the power of our spiritual and mental activity depends on the activity of our metabolic system. For example, if we eat too much or too little consciousness is difficult to maintain properly. Our 'light of consciousness' is like the flame that can only illuminate due to a process of destruction. The nourishing foundation for this flame of consciousness is the metabolic system within us. There the nourishing substances are destroyed, 'dismembered,' thereby releasing their life-forces so they can serve as the foundation for consciousness. We are able to think because of the 'destructive furnace' in our bodily nature. Our thinking is to begin with a 'breaking down,' a distinguishing or separation. It requires special effort to move beyond that kind of thinking to thought that synthesizes, unites, combines to create, rather than take apart.

These destructive forces within us can also become active beyond our consciousness (thinking) and into our feeling and willing. Then they become the foundation for antipathy in the soul and an impulse towards evil. One can think of metabolism as antipathy at work in the body. Substances are not allowed *in the form they are constituted outside the body*, to become the flesh of the body. They must firstly be completely destroyed; only then can some portion of them be absorbed into our body.[6] In this process we have a picture of forces within us that will not allow any significance to anything foreign, that wants only itself, its 'own.' This, of course, is antipathy in the soul.

We see how deeply evil branches out in us. Here too the positive as well as the negative roles of evil become visible. We are dealing with a powerful force, which works to break down and destroy in the metabolism and even makes conscious knowledge possible through a thinking activity that can analyse (from Greek *ana* = down and *lysis* = break). However, this force can do monstrous things when it breaks out of human beings un-mastered and uncontrolled.

Many of the terrible and inhuman deeds perpetrated in our time are only comprehensible as the effects of these destructive forces unleashed from their proper place in the human metabolic system. The kind of thinking done today, abstract and with little heart involvement, cannot do justice to the process of life. This thinking, that splits and analyses, not only involves antipathetic forces, as indicated above, but also involves unconquered forces of death and destruction, that manifest themselves as inimical to life and are intensely destructive for the earth and humanity. The best example of this is the construction and use of the atomic bomb.

The forces that, at first, bring about good in the body prove to be fatal when they become not only the *foundation* of our consciousness and our thinking, but actually determine the course and quality of that conscious activity. If divisive, analytic, broken down, destructive and dead thinking is not enlivened by a united, combining, formative, synthesizing and, above all, life-fostering kind of thinking, if we do not consciously set the powers of devotion and love next to the forces of antipathy in the soul, then the destructive forces set free from the body will only bring more evil into the world.

Something of this fact, which is deeply bound up with our human being, is expressed in the Act of Consecration of Man during Passion Tide when the seasonal prayer speaks of 'the sting of evil' in the human heart. Paul also uses this image when he says, 'And to keep me from being too elated by the abundance of revelations, a thorn was given me in the flesh, a messenger from Satan ...' (2Cor.12:7 JM). Or when we hear in the Lord's prayer, 'deliver us from evil.' When Christianity speaks of our need for redemption it is not least due to the far reaching state of affairs connected with the forces mentioned here.

In the chapter concerning the origin of evil we spoke of man's significance for the world. From that point of view we can consider the following: if all-encompassing future possibilities are intended for man then we must not 'think small' when we consider the possibilities for evil that is so intertwined with mankind. We can interpret and understand evil as the deeply planted 'thorn' meant to stimulate us to call up all available forces to deal with the challenge presented by the enormity of evil.

The events of the last century and the start of the present allow no doubt that the abyss does exist and can open at any time, that is, something that actually should be described as 'pathological' threatens to become 'normal.' Today and in the future this threatens the very qualities we call human. We should not underestimate it. Will there be a medicine for this kind of illness?

We now have seen that the Adversaries' work is not restricted to the human soul, but is able to reach into the deeper levels of our humanity. In the next chapter we will consider this state of affairs further.

CHAPTER 8

Deeper Consequences of the Fall

Original sin

Since Augustine (AD 354–430) the concept of 'original sin' has played an important role in Christianity. This idea sees any individual as already guilty and sinful before they commit any sin in the here and now. Even a newborn child is afflicted by inherited sinfulness. From this point of view, the condition of man is not dependent upon his own will and behaviour; he is born as a sinner.

This fact goes back to the sin of Adam. All of humanity sinned 'in him.' As a result of Adam's sin we are all worthy of damnation. In theology and Church practice this view has played a significant and not always happy role. The consequences of this view have proven problematic. Augustine, in particular, set forth a theory that claims that our future is pre-destined by an absolute God. The question of ultimate salvation or damnation is also intimately connected with this flawed idea of original sin. Anthroposophy, the spiritual science developed by Rudolf Steiner, offers a necessary correction to this view and a reasonable explanation of what lies behind it.

The many levels of the human being

According to spiritual science there are many levels of being in humans.[1] Man is not at all a simple being. In ancient times it was thought that humans are made up of three parts: a body, a soul (or spirit), and a differentiated soul-spiritual part. Anthroposophy allows us to understand man in an even more differentiated way, yet clearly and concretely.

Firstly, today the *earthly, material body* is the only object of scientific research. Its existence is indubitable. For anthroposophic observation, however, the physical body is only the lowest 'member.' No judgment or valuation is intended by the use of the word 'lowest.' Further regions or aspects of the human being can be named and described. They constitute further 'members' or levels of the human being (which could also be called aspects, processes or functions) and represent a 'higher' bodily character. They can also be thought of as 'husks' or 'sheaths' within which the human self can function on these various higher levels. Secondly, the next such member is the *life-forces* which permeate our earthly body. These form a 'finer body' within the material body. One can speak of the 'life body' or 'etheric body' as the second member of the human constitution. These life-forces enliven the physical body; without them it would be dead. They take care of growth, nourishment, regeneration, mobility; they are the foundation of all health and illness, but also for our bodily sense of well-being. The forces of life do not originate in the physical body. At death they withdraw from the body. Like humans, plants and animals also have a life body as opposed to minerals, which do not. Thirdly, in humans and also in animals there is a third member: the region of soul-forces called the 'soul body' or 'astral body.' (Astral because its substance is derived from the stars). This is also an independent realm, a separate level in the human being, that does not originate in the physical or life bodies.

All the forces in the soul that come from the region of instincts, passions, etc., which human beings in a certain way have in common with animals, belong to the soul-forces. Beyond these, thinking, feeling, and will in human beings also belong to the soul body.

Just as the life body leaves the body at death, so does the soul body. During sleep the soul body also lifts out of the physical body almost entirely. Through this withdrawal the physical body falls into unconsciousness. In sleep it is 'plant like,' in the sense that it is permeated only by the life body. The soul body (and 'I') are united with the spiritual world in sleep.

The 'I'

We have described three levels or members of human nature:
— physical body (like minerals);
— life-forces / life body / etheric body (like plants);
— soul-forces / soul body / astral body (like animals).

With the 'I', the human being rises an additional level above the animal. This is the fourth member of man's being, which man alone possesses. The other three members are more *external*; they constitute his 'sheaths.' The 'I' is the kernel of the human self, the individual, unique, 'one-of-a-kindness' belonging to every human being. The 'I' makes us into an incomparable and irreplaceable being in the universe.

This 'I' is eternal and has come forth out of the Godhead as a 'spark' from the divine fire, as a 'drop' out of the ocean of God. This eternal being lives in the sheaths of the other three members and it is — if we use the idea of reincarnation — incarnated again and again through many earthly lives, in varied life circumstances, with changing characteristics and different gender, alternating male and female incarnations.

Proceeding from one incarnation to another as an 'I'-being we learn to advance from a childlike, naïve, dependent relationship to an independent, self-aware and responsible existence. The question of destiny, of human freedom and evil, is connected with the 'I'. These are questions that have no meaning for an animal because an animal has no 'I'. In the beginning we had an entirely different character. The original human being was radically changed through the Fall into sin. To understand this change more completely and to better grasp the working of the Adversaries within it, we will now consider paradisal man and then, once again, the Fall.

The origin of man

Humans first emerged from the Godhead as purely spiritual beings. That means that our 'I', as the divine within us, was surrounded by sheaths that were still entirely permeated by spirit. They were also not-individualized and childlike. Pure devotion to the divine lived in the *soul-forces*, without fear and without any kind of egotism, but also without any self-awareness or independent knowledge. The *life-forces* were undiminished by sickness or weakness but were also without any individualization. What we today call our *physical body*, was at that time, just like a breath of air, entirely unearthly, not yet material.

There are three distinct stages of creation that can be distinguished in the Old Testament:

1. The purely spiritual creation found in the first chapter of Genesis where nothing earthly or even material is present, only the ideas for the whole of creation are brought forward;

2. The actual creation of the earth that signifies the beginning of 'embodiment' found in chapter two of Genesis;
3. The hardening of earthly existence and the human body brought on by the Fall into sin; only at this last, third stage can we speak of solid matter that exists as a *contradiction* to the spiritual.

In the beginning, we appeared as paradisal, unearthly beings, united with God in a childlike way. Without sin or any evil we were also without freedom or knowledge.

However, in this state we were still the 'peak' of creation, the 'image and likeness of God.' In an undeveloped yet germinal way, paradisal man lived this mystery. This unevolved state pushed for development: creative freedom, self-awareness and responsibility, self-knowledge and the world, as aids for self-education and development, were to be awakened in man. The Adversaries were called upon to serve as an impulse for human destiny and evolution.

The poisoning of human nature

Lucifer gained access to the paradisal, pre-earthly human being. Not only one man but all of mankind was affected. The snake is a mythical picture for Lucifer; paradise is a mythical picture for the world of origin of the childlike human being. The figure of Adam also has mythological-imaginative content; he is not simply 'a human being' or the 'ancestor' of all mankind in an earthly sense. He is a picture or archetype of all mankind, in which every human being participates.

'In Adam' we are all created out of the being of God. As a mythological picture, Adam stands for every human being. We have all felt the influence of 'the snake.' From this point of view, Augustine's idea, that all human beings have experienced the Fall into sin 'in Adam,' acquires its true meaning.

Now, how are we to understand this Luciferic influence? In the true sense of the word: influence means 'in-flow.' Lucifer's power flowed into the soul body of humans. The soul-forces were stirred up by Lucifer to form a wish, a desire for the 'apple' in terms of doubt ('did God say'), of egotism ('you will be like God'). At the beginning, the immediate consequences of the Fall are of a psychological nature, not yet physical: only fear, shame, need for protection.

The 'I', that was free and devoted to God was, through the Fall, drawn into the soul body and covered over, buried by increasingly egotistical soul-forces. The consequence was a severe change in the I's experience of itself. Until then we could feel ourselves to be pure and childlike as part of the world, and experience other human beings as equally significant. We now begin to experience ourselves as the centre of the world; the world revolves only around us. All that is outside of us is periphery and, therefore, ultimately has only peripheral significance. We can hardly do other than experience the world in a selfish, subjective way. The 'I,' originally comprised of pure spirit, is buried by egotistical soul-forces and therefore takes on characteristics of the soul: it becomes 'soul-like' while the soul becomes 'I-like.' This means that the actions of the 'I,' which should be free and motivated by the spirit, betrays motives that originate in the personal, egotistical soul. And the soul, which should serve the 'I' that is spiritually above it, asserts its own personal desires taking over the centre of the human being where only the 'I' should be directing human actions.[2]

In light of the consequences of the Fall, which are to be seen as a poisoning of the entire human being at all levels, it is important to remember that this evolution is a part of a great, positive goal. In reality the process of the Fall described here took place slowly over extensive periods of time. Indeed, the Fall does represent a specific point in time, but its consequences unfolded only gradually over time. Also, what is described in the Bible which may appear as an affair of a few moments is, in reality, a matter of longer periods of time.

Ageing, death, hardening of the earth

The consequences of the Fall did not end with the Luciferic influence on the soul-forces and the 'soul body.' The Luciferic influence drew in the Ahrimanic after it. After Lucifer found access to the human being, Ahriman could follow. His work transforms not only the soul, but also the life-forces and above all the physical body.

The physical body is, therefore, becoming increasingly earthly, actually material. Only now does the body become a place of pain, of bodily torture. And, because of its progressive hardening — we call this 'ageing'— after a series of years the body becomes so unusable by the 'I' that it must leave and death occurs.

The Fall has another, even more encompassing consequence.

Repercussions affect not only man's bodily nature, hardening it, but also the 'bodily nature' of the earth itself. The entire physical earth is included in the hardening process.

We find this fact reflected in the Bible with the words '... cursed is the ground because of you; in toil you shall eat of it all the days of your life; thorns and thistles it shall bring forth to you; ... In the sweat of your face you shall eat bread ...' (Gen.3:17–19 RSV). This passage is telling us two things.

Firstly, the imperfection of the earthly, finite world is connected to the Fall of man. With this Fall, man has taken the entire world with him. In this way the earthly world bears the imprint of the Fall into sin with itself and also needs salvation. This is the meaning of Paul's words in his Letter to the Romans:

> All around us creation waits with great longing that the sons of
> God shall begin to shine forth in mankind. Creation has become
> transitory, not through its own doing, but because of him who,
> becoming transitory himself, dragged it down with him, and
> therefore everything in it is full of longing for the future. For
> the breath of freedom will also waft through the kingdoms of
> creation; the tyranny of transitory existence will cease ...We
> know that the whole of creation suffers and sighs in the pangs
> of a new birth until the present day.' (Rom.7:19–22 JM).

In his Fall, man brought creation down with him: 'cursed is the ground because of you.' Yet creation will be redeemed again in the future from 'the tyranny of transitory existence' — according to Paul — through the salvation of the human being.

Secondly, if the report of creation speaks of man's task and promise to 'fill the earth and subdue it' (Gen.1:28) then after the Fall the 'curse of work' is united with the earthly destiny of man: 'In the sweat of your face you shall eat bread.'

The fact that we must work in order to live on the earth is connected with the Fall. Our enslavement to physical work (the effect of Ahriman) signifies a terrible oppression for all humanity, a heavy burden for millions of people.

We see the deleterious effects of the Fall into sin in three levels:
— the '*I*' is bound to the soul; it appears in the egotism of the soul as the 'lower self,' entirely concerned with itself.

— the *soul body* with all the forces of the soul are permeated by egotism by Lucifer; it becomes 'I-like.'
— the *physical body* of the human being becomes material and hardened through Ahriman's intervention. Ageing and death are immediate consequences. An additional, crucial consequence is the
hardening of the earth as it becomes merely transitory.

Sickness, suffering, and infirmity

Ahriman is the one who darkens and afflicts life-forces with disease.
This is the source of all physical illness and bodily infirmities. In a sense,
ageing is also caused by this, for the hardening of the physical body
interacts with the weakness of those life-forces that permeate the physical body. This interaction intensifies the deleterious effects of each.

Originally, human life-forces were free and creative in the physical
body which was not yet earthly. In paradise we did not know illness
or hunger, we were not burdened by bodily passions or ill humour; for
the life-forces holding sway over the physical body worked in such a
way that the eye and soul of the human being was not burdened by the
processes taking place in the life sphere. All of this changed because of
the influence from Ahriman. The life-forces of the human being were
robbed of their free creative power and became weak and susceptible
to illness. They were unable to regenerate themselves indefinitely. In
this way, countless possibilities for sickness and infirmity arose with
accompanying suffering. There is hardly anyone alive today who is
spared all of this. Our susceptibility and dependency in this realm was
caused by the Fall into sin.

Hunger and thirst

Through the influence of Ahriman the life body lost its ability to regenerate the human organization. This resulted in the human need to take
in nourishment from outside the body and we became dependent on
food taken from the environment. This is one of the most tragic consequences of the Fall. What it means is that we are thus tied to the earth
through hunger and thirst which, consequently, have been responsible
for so much suffering.

Furthermore, passion in the human soul has united with the process
of bodily nourishment. Combined with the purely physical drive and

compulsion to eat, this passionate desire for pleasure has brought about an even stronger binding of the soul to the body. In this way, Lucifer enters into that which Ahriman has awakened. There he finds his own advantage and begins his work. In the next area to be discussed, we will see how the two Adversaries work together in the consequences of the Fall.

It is true that in many areas of the world today the earth (including the animal world) is not able to produce enough nourishment for humanity. When it comes to nourishment, we have no choice but to be egotistical; for what one human being claims for himself is no longer available for any other. We are compelled to be egotistical. In this field the Adversaries have bound to human beings so completely that hardly any escape is possible. Of course, we do not mean to say anything against the natural joy to be found in eating and drinking. However, the tragedy of the physical body's compelling power over us and the seductive power of pleasure cannot be overlooked. In light of third-world hunger, many people find themselves confronted with questions when offered by a sumptuous five-course meal. Illness and the need for material nourishment are two of Ahriman's greatest effects in the human life body, but there are two additional consequences that must be also considered. Firstly, the fact that certain processes in the human soul are now bound to the bodily nature and secondly, the fact that the human ability to perceive the world clearly has been darkened.

The first consequence concerns our dependency on the body for certain moods and even for our sense of well-being. Certain bodily organs can, for example, bring about severe depression. The human being is unable to free himself from depression even though it is *only* a consequence of bodily processes. In our souls we are chained to our body and un-free; it is difficult, if not impossible, to work against a mood that has been created in the body. This is a consequence of Ahriman's power.

The human being: masculine – feminine

If we look back at the paradisal human being, we find in the biblical report an astonishing fact: Adam — the human being — is, to begin with, a unified being. He was created by God as both a masculine and feminine being. The masculine forces and feminine forces are united. Only later is the feminine removed from the whole human being (not masculine, not male) which is Adam. Eve then stands over and against Adam who now lacks the feminine component (Gen.2). Man and woman arise then as one-sided extremes of the original human being which was masculine - feminine.

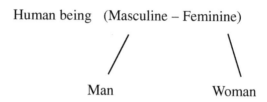

Human being (Masculine – Feminine)

Man   Woman

Therefore man and woman, are one-sided variations of the original unified human being. One could say that in the masculine, the man, we have an Ahrimanic one-sidedness and in the feminine, woman, a Luciferic one-sidedness. In their basic nature, neither male nor female are fully human; both must strive for the fully human. Only then can they grow out of their respective forms of one-sidedness.

Knowledge of the many layers, or levels, to be found in the human being can be informative for us here. For the differences that determine sex concern the physical body and, beyond that, also the life body; in the soul body men and women are no longer specifically gender-orientated. Of course, the soul qualities of men and women today appear as one-sided masculine or feminine traits. However, the more spiritual forces become active in the soul, the more balanced and mature the human being becomes, to overcome the one-sidedness of sex, the more he or she becomes fully 'human.'

Only soul-forces bound to the body, for example, sexual instincts, display unambiguously the determining characteristics of one sex. The 'I,' above all, stands beyond the connection to one sex. The higher forces of the human being may live in a gender specific body but can nevertheless be free of that body.

Human beings today are learning increasingly to experience themselves as 'I'-beings and not merely as the 'role' assigned to their sex. Hence, the problem of equality between the sexes has become acute in our time, and properly so. With respect to higher human forces men and women are completely equal. There is a spiritual objectivity in the movement for women's rights and sexual equality, which has led to a Christian priesthood in which women can participate fully, for example, in the Christian Community since 1922.

On the other hand, it must be stressed that women cannot achieve the fully human condition (balance between masculine and feminine) simply by becoming one-sided on the masculine side. The decisive step lies precisely in the harmony between the two forces, not in women denying their feminine side as the feminine also belongs to our full humanity.

This process of achieving a balanced, full humanness is aided by reincarnation. As a rule, male and female incarnations alternate. Someone who is living a life today as a woman will likely incarnate in their next life as a man and vice versa. Indeed, this need for balance points to the necessity for repeated earth lives. The one-sidedness caused by gender in one lifetime can be balanced out in the next.

In the Bible, the separation of the sexes occurs before the Fall into sin. This implies that one-sided gender qualities and the differences between man and woman must still belong to the order of paradise and, in and of themselves, are a good thing and not a problem. However, it is clear that the separation of the sexes provided an opening for Lucifer and hence the Fall. When Eve stands next to Adam, the human being is already polarized. The creative tension between them, which includes the instincts, is the place where Lucifer and Ahriman work together to lead us away from our full humanity.

The bite into the apple

The Fall into sin, the 'bite into the apple' is usually interpreted in a one-sided way as the Fall into sexuality. However, much more than just sexuality is connected with the Fall. The question of sexuality is only part of the problem. For modern humans though, it is certainly of the greatest significance and has forced itself into the foreground, and is connected with weighty questions and burdens for everyone today.

Lucifer's seduction of mankind is connected with a turning away from the spirit towards the earthly. This fact appears in the mythological-imaginative picture of 'eating the hidden fruit' that is ripening on the 'tree of knowledge' in the garden of paradise. There is no mention of any apple (Gen.1:3). Nevertheless, visualizing the fruit of the tree of knowledge in the picture of an apple does correspond to the imaginative content of the process. Among the members of the rose family the apple has the most earthly character, not only because of its shape, but also because of the fundamental principle at work in its formation. The fruit is formed differently from other fruits in that the ovule sinks ever 'deeper' into the stem tissue that is being transformed into the flesh of the fruit. This is an image of the Fall of man but also of the fact that this Fall is to become fruitful.[3] One can see the apple as a picture of the earth itself, ripening on the world tree. We must be careful not to eat it too soon. Among ancient symbols for royal power we find the 'orb of kings,' a sphere representing the earth with a cross on it.

The bite into the apple is a pictorial expression of mankind's seduction by the snake, of our involvement with the earth. Within the framework of the event we find the phenomenon of human sexuality as a part of the whole. One is missing the point of the Fall into sin if sexuality itself is seen as the actual sin, as the primary content of the Fall. When the psychological experience of sexuality is weighted in this way it can lead to no good.

On the other hand it cannot be denied that the reproductive forces are among the most significant available to human beings. These are forces capable of creating, forming and shaping in that they can conceive and produce a complete human body.

It is one of the greatest wonders on earth that the union of a sperm cell and an egg cell can result in a human organism — a human organism able to receive a human 'I', and then carry it and its accompanying destiny for an entire human lifetime within a short period of time. We can only stand in amazement and reverence before this wonder. The only reason why we do not feel the wonder and sacredness of this process every time it occurs is because we have become insensitive through materialistic prejudice and habits of thought.

In the ability to procreate we carry the highest powers of creativity. They are like an after-image or reflection of God's own creative power, which brought forth humans in the begining. Just as God brought forth man in his own image and likeness, so the human being is able to beget descendants in his image and likeness. We carry a creative potential within us that is both a gift and a task at the same time.

This creative potential is not available for our use in a free way, but it is connected to bodily processes — glandular processes, hormonal secretions, etc. Stirrings in the soul (psychological impulses) are also connected to these processes: desire as an expression of 'instinctive tension.' These sensations and feelings do not freely rise up out of the body; they appear with compelling force. Then they can be taken hold of by egotism and become more powerful if appropriate self-education does not set in to regulate and transform these forces.

Of course, the Ahrimanic and Luciferic powers also enter this realm where they play off one another. Ahriman works to bind the creative forces of the life body (which are otherwise free), to the physiological process of the physical body, especially the male and female reproductive organs. Lucifer works to raise up into consciousness the purely physical-physiological processes that might have remained unconscious in the body, e.g. blood circulation and breathing, so that they are experienced in the soul as sexual desire, as instinctual impulses, as the drive for pleasure. Unconscious forces are intensified into consciousness of self and magnify the experience of self.

Sexuality

Just as a disturbance in the metabolism of the liver can lead to depression, so the elevation of the 'hormone level' in the blood can lead to sexual tension. In as much as egotistical, selfish inclinations of the soul unite with this process, the human being is more or less in the hands of the Adversaries. They have once again managed to draw noble human creative powers into their field of action.

We can see how powerful these forces are when we consider the fact that over 200 million sperm cells are produced every day in the male organism. This 'potency' (Latin for 'power') presents an enormous task for the human being who does not wish simply to surrender himself to the instinctive forces rising up out of his body, but wants to control and form them with his 'I.' Anyone who has taken on this task is dealing with powerful forces that are actually at home in the highest spiritual realm yet are now attached to the body.

It is a real question whether the cramped effort to behave in an 'uncramped' way in the field of sexuality does not actually create more problems. The biblical statement that shame followed the Fall into sin, points beyond its own context to: 'They saw that they were naked and sewed fig leaves together and made themselves aprons' (Gen.3:7 RSV). Sexuality proceeds without human fulfilment if it is not accompanied by responsibility and love of another human being, i.e., if it does not lead to 'knowledge'.

Sexuality without genuine fulfilment is always accompanied by shame; and shame is nothing more than the feeling that overcomes humans when they realize that their behaviour lies below the level of the human. Today, the objection that hardly anyone knows shame anymore is valid only in a limited sense; it may be true at the level of conscious experience but the deeper levels of the human being are not deceived. Those levels answer with a feeling of inner emptiness and profound dissatisfaction, which can be covered over for a time only by even greater sensations.

Previously we have spoken of the illusions with which Lucifer surrounds human desire. The field of sexual desire is saturated by such illusions that constantly arise anew.

Blindness

The effects of Ahriman's work are to be seen in the darkening of human sense-perceptions. The report of the Fall in the Bible includes this consequence: 'Their eyes were opened and they saw that they were naked ...' (RSV)

Clearly, opening the eyes means that they were able to perceive the physical world and see the 'naked facts' of earthly nature. This would imply that their perception before the Fall was of a different sort. An echo of this earlier method of perception still exists in small children. Returning to a place where we lived as a child is usually deeply disappointing. Somewhere in our memory we still have the golden glow of childhood that suffused everything at the physical location of our childhood. But now the same house, garden, street and trees appear, to the adult who sees them again, in an entirely earthly, austere light, as ordinary, everyday, 'naked.'

The predominance of the physical world as it gradually overwhelmed all other perceptions occurred with the Fall into sin — an event which, as we have said occurred over a very long stretch of time. Lucifer turned man towards the earth; Ahriman saw to it that the earthly would eventually appear in its material form only, stripped of all spirituality.

What did Adam and Eve see before their perception was darkened and their eyes were opened for the earthly alone? Their vision was not limited to the material part of nature and of the human being. They beheld themselves 'en-sheathed,' that is, surrounded by higher, undimmed forces of life and soul. The physical body seemed to have the weight of a breath of air, not yet material; as such it was present only in the background of what they perceived. Adam and Eve saw the aura of their whole human-being before it was darkened by the Fall.

As a result of the Fall this kind of seeing faded away. Humans found themselves as purely earthly beings unable to see into the spiritual world. The fact that we are blind to the spiritual is one of the essential consequences of the Fall. It is impossible to grasp the full extent of the effect this blindness has on human life. It is primarily because of this blindness that human beings became earthly beings without any connection to heaven and were thus exposed to Adversaries.

With this achievement, the Adversaries attained their first goal. At almost every level of their being humans have become a product of the Fall into sin. We no longer even know what we have lost.

The sickness of sin

We have seen that the Fall is an event that has taken hold of the entire human being. We can speak of a 'poisoning' of human nature. We are born into this situation. The consequences of the Fall, which sit within the human constitution, are inherited from generation to generation. We are not offered the choice of avoiding them.
— Our body is earthly, material, it gets old and dies
— Our life-forces are weakened and subject to sickness, suffering, hunger, thirst, and sexuality.
— Our soul-forces are not free but inordinately attached to our self-awareness. They are in part bound to our earthly-material body, dependent on hormones and other physiological processes.
— Our 'I' is, to begin with, experienced only as the lower 'I,' i.e., lower self.
— Our senses are limited to the physical world; blind to the spiritual.

Now we can see that Augustine, with his notion of 'original sin,' was not far from the truth. However, we must not think of 'original sin' as referring in a one-sided way only to sexuality, but rather to the entire situation given to a human being incarnating into the human hereditary line.

This existential predicament is spoken of in the creed of the Christian Community with the term 'Sickness of Sin,' which takes us away from the old expression, 'original sin.' The concept of 'sickness' corrects the moralizing one-sidedness of the word 'sin,' a correction necessary and appropriate for our time. This is not to say that individual sin and error do not exist or should not be evaluated morally. The 'sickness of sin' refers to the basic human disposition which is permeated by the consequences of the Fall like a sickness. Furthermore, right now we are unable to do anything about this fact. This basic disposition, present in all humans, precedes any individual sin.

Sickness requires healing and medication. We will see how, in a wonderful way, some medications arise from the sickness itself. However, other medications must be added. Therefore, we next consider Christ, the physician and healer of mankind.

CHAPTER 9

Man: Good or Evil

Now that we have an overview of our cosmic and earthly situation, the question arises: what can be said of man that is good? Are we not forced to ascribe to him a radical state of evil? Are there perhaps ways to overcome this situation?

We come from above

To answer these questions, we need to complete the previously-presented picture of the various levels that exist in man. The 'I' is actually called upon to rule over and direct the other members of the human constitution. Instead, because of the Fall, it has lost its authority and has fallen under the sway of the soul-forces that have become egotistical. The 'I' is not master in his own house. The Adversaries are not actually located in the 'I' itself, but in the other members with the result that the 'I' is not free and sovereign in what actually belongs to it. Hence, it has become 'lower self,' trapped in subjectivity and self-absorption.

Nevertheless, another world shines into this 'I.' The human being as previously described is incomplete. We have described him 'from below' so to speak. It is characteristic of humans to strive for more; more of all things but also good things like wisdom, patience and beauty. We must not overlook the fact that behind this striving lies a force that can lead us above and beyond ourselves. From above, so to speak, something shines into human life and destiny that is not already contained in the lower members but that can be taken up by them. For our 'I' does not come from below; it comes with birth out of a higher existence, out of a pre-earthly, spiritual world into the earthly. From there it brings an echo of what was experienced in the spiritual world.

The small child is still perceptibly surrounded by the breath of the spirit. There is something still heavenly about the child that any open-minded person can sense. But this shimmer of spiritual glory soon vanishes. It moves inwards illuminating us from within. The ideals in the soul, the striving for truth, beauty and goodness — for compassion and understanding of other human beings — are not merely an echo, but evidence, of the activity of a higher world within the human soul. The question of the meaning of one's own destiny and of existence altogether is like a dawning memory that one has worked on the meaning of one's life (and therefore also the world) in the spiritual world before birth. This is also true for the feeling of responsibility for our own actions.

We have already pointed out that there must be some kind of yardstick or criterion within us, a basic knowledge and a feeling for good and evil, without which insight into the moral significance of our actions would not be possible. There actually are some people who lack this measure — a psychological anomaly. Good itself actually extends into our soul with such insights. Now it is clear that we are dealing here with a continuing effect of our pre-birth experience. In the spiritual world before the start of our earthly lives we experienced truth, beauty and goodness, not as moral demands but rather as realities. More accurately stated: we *lived* in truth, beauty and goodness in the spiritual world. When we came to earth we brought a measure of uprightness with us.

The higher 'I'

After pointing out the existence of this realm of ideals within us we can go a step further. What we have in a human incarnated on the earth is only a part of human reality. To every earthly human there belongs another part, a spiritual part that does not enter into earthly incarnation, yet is united with our earthly destiny. It is a part of our own true being, our higher 'I' or 'higher self,' our eternal part that hovers above us, that is far away and yet near to us. This higher self is not subject to the attack of the Adversaries and is, therefore, not fully present in earthly man.

Nevertheless, the higher 'I' is constantly sending impulses to the human being that belongs to it on earth. These impulses come to life in us as ideals, in the search for meaning, in feelings of responsibility, and as that which we *really* want to do. We have the freedom to turn to this region of our being or not. Our conscience, in particular, is connected with our higher self.

Unconsciously, every night when we are asleep we turn to our higher self. The 'I' that is incarnated on earth leaves its body every night in sleep and ascends to the spiritual world. There it encounters its higher being which seeks to give it strength for the coming day. To be sure, this strength can only become effective in waking consciousness to the extent that the we devote ourselves not only to external, material life, but also consciously to seeking the spiritual on earth. Our conscious turning to the spirit allows our higher self to radiate into our lower self — into our earthly personality. Our higher self works not only in the concrete realm of ideals, not only in sleep and in our conscious attention to the spiritual world, but also intensely in shaping our destiny.

The choice of destiny by the higher self

With genuine insight into destiny today we realize that destiny is not simply dropped on top of us by an external power. It is an error to imagine that we had no part in forming it. Of course, it may look that way from the point of view of earthly consciousness, which would lead us to say: I have no idea what will come tomorrow, I don't know why this or that blow of destiny has befallen me. Our consciousness in earthly life is darkened — certainly for our own good, for we would lose all openness and freedom in our actions if we could foresee our destiny.

However, the situation is different before we set out on our earthly incarnation. From our higher self we have insight into the earthly life ahead of us and into the forces of destiny connected with us. We know which experiences are necessary for us in our coming life, what we must do to balance past guilt, which forms of suffering have been necessitated by past misconduct. But we also know what will challenge and foster our spiritual growth, what we must expect of ourselves and what help will be available. However, destiny is not simply 'set in stone' in our pre-earthly existence; it can be shaped further and modified during life on earth. We realize during our life in the spiritual world before birth that painful experiences are also among the factors that foster spiritual growth. Meister Eckhart said, 'Suffering is the fastest horse that will carry us to perfection.'

When preparing for incarnation our view of our upcoming life is completely unsentimental. We are in agreement with the plans for our destiny. In our true self we want this destiny and it is this wanting alone that leads us to earth, not blind fate. A human embryo would not even be conceived on earth if a soul did not want to be born on earth.

There are many more questions associated with the theme of human intentions before birth. What about the destiny of criminals? Is it already predestined that an individual will be a criminal? Perhaps it has already become clear that individuals may not want to avoid troubled destinies precisely because they can learn the most from them. Furthermore, the evil or good (even good!) done in one life does not decide the ultimate goodness or evil of the whole person. The will towards a particular illness, towards poverty or weakness of any kind may be part of our pre-earthly intentions because of the experiences and opportunities that can only be learned in that way. This is true even though in our present consciousness we are not at all aware of it. My desire before birth for certain experiences continues to live in my higher self. I am blind to it only in my earthly consciousness.

In forming destiny for my next lifetime not only is the question asked, 'What do I need to do in order to balance past guilt?' but also the question: 'What abilities do I need to acquire for future tasks?' Our higher self aims towards the future. There is a calling that reaches us from the future. It too plays an important role in the question of destiny so that the meaning of our present life also is derived from the future. Therefore, much of what we experience and suffer is not the consequence of previous lives but rather preparation in anticipation of future tasks. It is a training for future abilities and apparent 'gifts.'

Many destinies of our time only make sense when seen from this point of view. There may not be a single difficult and unhappy destiny today that does not have a future destiny shining into it. This idea may prevent us from assuming past guilt in ourselves — or others — when we see ourselves, or others, in a difficult, pain-filled destiny. There are, indeed, points of view that help us to believe in the meaningful progress of life on earth, and that encourage us to bear the burden of what must be carried.

These ideas also illuminate destinies that may appear to be without any meaning, were it not for the idea of reincarnation. I am thinking of the developmentally disabled whose physical and mental abilities leave them without any prospect for a normal life. Anthroposophically-inspired education for special needs, which is based on the idea of reincarnation, has achieved amazing results with the severely disabled. The conviction that such lives have a profound spiritual and karmic significance leads to new possibilities in education that have been extraordinarily successful. There is no doubt that the awareness that such human souls also have a future is not an illusion, but shows itself to be the most practical and only help for these people. Destinies of this sort, which may appear to be totally without value in this lifetime, may well have been designed to create new soul capacities for the individual in his next lifetime.

Our destiny is the result of our higher self shaping and directing our lives. This higher self wants to guide us through all the suffering and trials, through all the temptations we must endure to eventually achieve good. Above all, when we encounter our higher 'I' during sleep, our will for good, which is revealed in our destiny, is encouraged and reunited with the power for good in our life. And so we ask the question again, is man good or evil?

Man: the twofold being

A preliminary answer: Evil, as Luciferic and Ahrimanic forces, appears in the lower members of man in such a way that incarnated humans could not exist without them. We are inseparably linked with evil, as we have seen, even in the deepest levels of our bodily existence. On the other hand, in our earthly lives good extends into us 'from above.' *This good belongs to our true nature more profoundly than evil.* Nevertheless, good is only given to us on earth when we acquire it in freedom and make it real ourselves. Because of the nature of the fallen world evil is necessarily present in humans. Good, except when it is a childlike goodness, is only present if we ourselves call it forth and struggle for it.

In doing good we are working with our innermost forces, whereas when we carry out evil actions we are never quite 'ourselves.' In our discussion of destiny, we saw that the power of good shines into our own 'I', as it were, from above and at the same time it approaches us from outside in the workings of destiny, but here too it lies within our human freedom to accept these workings or to ignore them.

We see man as a double being: deeply connected with evil — in the Bible we read, 'for the imagination of man's heart is evil from his youth' (Gen.8:21 RSV) On the other hand, man is much more deeply and originally connected with good than with evil because his actual being originates in good. Hence, God could say after creating the human being, 'and behold, it was very good' (Gen.1:31).

This original goodness is also found in human beings who appear to be 'only' evil. In these people too there is an 'I' struggling to stand upright. Considered in the light of repeated earth lives, this struggle has hope even if everything in this life appears hopeless. Furthermore, the reverse is also true: there is evil even in the noblest, best human beings. We are all struggling for good. What are the prospects for a positive outcome?

CHAPTER 10

Overcoming Evil

The self (the 'I'), and the soul (the astral-forces), of humans are entry portals for Luciferic temptation, yet there are measures that can be taken to battle evil in these two areas.

Motivation for good

Our true 'I' has fallen under the influence of soul-forces that are egotistical and fear-filled, thereby becoming the *lower* 'I'. However, there are also forces streaming down into our lower, earthly self from the higher self which can guide us. What are the conditions that strengthen these forces and help us to shape our earthly lives more consciously? Expressed differently: how can our lower self, that lives in the sphere of egotism and fear, be strengthened and helped so that it can again do justice to its true role as 'master of the house' and as mediator between the earthly and spiritual worlds? There are two things that must be considered here.

— The human self, the 'I', needs a conscious orientation.

— The 'I' needs to be strengthened with will forces.

The first of these points we could designate as 'motivation for good.'

One of the most serious hindrances to the development of good in human beings today is the decline in values. What can we use for orientation? Does 'good' exist at all? Are not all standards merely relative and historically conditioned? If man is simply an evolved animal then how can we be held responsible for anything? If the earth is nothing more than a speck of dust in the infinite emptiness of space than how can my actions for good, or for evil, have any significance anyway?

Humans will always seek meaning beyond the materialistic interpretation of life because, in the depths of their souls they 'know' that meaning, truth and goodness exist, and that they must seek them.

Therefore, one of the most important preconditions for overcoming evil is knowledge of man and his evolution — especially in connection with evil — knowledge of the earth and the universe, of the spiritual world and of the being of God. Such knowledge is available today through anthroposophy, which is clear and understandable and reaches into the details of life.

Moral orientation in the past was provided by commandments and laws. These moral values were imposed by forces external to man and their decline has been progressing inexorably since about the middle of the twentieth century. This is a historical necessity, for we must learn to do good because we ourselves know what it is and love it, not because we fear punishment for overstepping a law external to us. In order to do this we need to know how we and our actions fit into the context of the universe. We need to know that man is not an insignificant something (or nothing) that the modern, materialistic worldview describes and *must* describe.

We need a meaningful picture of the world that is large and comprehensive enough to motivate us for good and to interest us in life. Such a world-picture would include heaven and earth, spirit and matter, good and evil. It is the first precondition for the human self to find an orientation in its struggle with evil. In contrast to this, a materialistic worldview necessarily leads to a narrowing of our view of the world and our lives; ultimately it leads to a loss of interest in life and an inability to see life's richness, in other words, it leads to greater egotism.

Above all, the activity of the 'I' consists of agreement or rejection, in saying yes or no, in an ongoing process of taking a position for oneself and to the world.[1] In the final analysis it is the 'I,' the self itself that rejects an evil deed or 'lets it in.' Of course, it is the same with good deeds. Görres formulates this fact as follows:

> We never find evil willed for the sake of evil. Not even the devil can do that. He who is evil, in order to be evil, finds the contradiction of evil to be a *good*. The motives are like all motives without exception: an understood value and form of goodness.[2]

But this means that we can only 'aim' for something good, i.e., something that appears to us as good. Not even the Adversaries can change this. However, they can darken and destroy our worldview so that, for a moment or fundamentally, something appears good or worth striving for, which, when seen in the light of a larger context, could be called anything but good.

An extreme example of this is seen in the deeds of a terrorist prepared to kill innocent people out of 'good intentions.' Good intentions in this case means that the deed appears as a positive achievement when seen against the background of his worldview. His ideal may be that of awakening people and liberating them. Against the background of this distorted and narrow view of the world, genuinely noble human ideals may give rise to incredibly destructive deeds. All revolutions involve such motivations. An excellent example is Robespierre and his actions during the French revolution; his 'incorruptible' ideals delivered countless people to the guillotine.

However, we do not need to look so far afield; within ourselves there are sufficient examples pointing in this direction. A 'good' is dangled before us and we agree to it, i.e., attach our 'I' to it. Here it is clear that the most important guide for good is knowledge. Accurate knowledge of man and the world can illuminate our view of the world allowing us to correct false notions and misplaced 'ideals,' thereby helping us to make better decisions. Shedding new light into our consciousness is then the first necessary step. Without this step there will be no overcoming of evil in the future. In other words, our 'I' is given its first decisive help in the battle against evil through the acquisition of a worldview that adequately accounts for the spiritual world as well as material, earthly existence.

Strengthening the 'I'

Furthermore, our striving for good is undermined not only by inadequate insight and lack of orientation, but also by the weakness and dullness of our earthly self. For it often happens that we assent to a less than moral deed despite knowing better. Such a decision, made by the 'I,' takes place as described above: for a moment we ascribe a higher value (happiness, pleasure, gain, honor, power, etc.) to a bad action than to what we actually know and feel to be the good. We can 'know' very well that we are doing something wrong; nevertheless we do wrong because momentarily it attracts us more powerfully. In this case, too, in the moment of decision when the 'I' assigns a higher value to something bad, it sees it as a 'good.'[3]

Here it is a question of having the strength to follow our insight or yielding to an object that appeals to our egotism. Fear also often plays a complicated role in such decisions. This is where most questions actually appear. This is where guilt arises.

When we act against our better insight in doing something wrong, immoral and egotistical, guilt is clearly created. The more damage done to other people and to ourselves, the greater the misfortune created by our deeds and the greater our guilt. The greatest questions of everyday life arise here. We must seek for sources of strength that can give to our 'I' qualities of strength, endurance and wakefulness, and that will work against egotism and fear.

The idea that evil can easily be overcome, that it is just a matter of 'good will' is an illusion. Mankind's entanglement with evil reaching back through the millennia cannot be undone in the wave of a hand. Our struggle with evil is not a quick war leading to a swift victory; it is more like protracted trench warfare or guerrilla warfare with brief victories. And certainly images taken from warfare are not even the best. In strengthening the 'I' we make progress not so much by battling against our weaknesses as by planting and cultivating better soul characteristics, i.e., by improving our character. A similar approach holds true for farming. Weeds are best eliminated not by the use of poisons, which ultimately immunize them and lead to more weeds, but by improving the desired plants and soil so that farmland becomes less susceptible to destructive plants.

In the human realm, it is also better to attend to the forces that can contribute to healing and strengthening the soul. First of all, let us mention those soul-forces that have not fallen to the Luciferic temptation, or not entirely, or that are easier to wrestle free from that temptation than others. We can call them 'spiritually-inclined' because they cause the spiritual elements within us to become active, the elements that lead us beyond the one-sided earthly, open us to the spiritual, and hence lift our 'I' into the vertical. In this way the 'I' is gradually restored to its original authority over the soul. These uplifting and strengthening forces are already connected to a view of the world that includes the spirit.

The new Adam

Instead of the images from battle used to describe the processes that lead to strengthening of the 'I' and overcoming of evil, we prefer pictures of 'building' and 'edification,' words which mean 'the process of instructing or improving spiritually.' 'Edify' comes from a Latin word meaning 'to build a house.' By connecting with spiritually-inclined forces and cultivating them in our souls we allow another human being to arise within us, a higher being related to the spirit. The 'old human being,' the one we are merely by virtue of the forces of nature within us, does not by any means immediately disappear. He will continue to make his presence felt. He cannot be killed. However, he does gradually lose his insistence on self when we observe that we are gradually growing into a new person. Paul created the concept of the 'old Adam' and the 'new Adam' (1Cor.15). He is saying that a future being can come alive in us and achieve reality as the new Adam, even if the old Adam does not cease to exist. (There is an old saying, 'I tried to drown my old Adam but it turns out he can swim.') In this regard there are two illusions to overcome. We tend to alternate between them or, according to temperament, *lean* towards one of them. The illusion that we could easily dispose with many of our weaknesses if we really tried reflects a Luciferic influence. The other illusion is that, even if we really tried, we could achieve nothing in this regard, and that it therefore doesn't really matter anyway. This is Ahrimanic cynicism that is especially fascinating. The truth is just the opposite. Whatever we can achieve in overcoming our weaknesses and in the development of positive soul-forces has enormous significance for us, even beyond our own lives.

What are the inner thoughts and feelings that will strengthen our 'I' in the way described? First of all, develop a loving interest in the world around you. Practising such an interest will weaken the chains on our 'I'; it will begin to dissolve our egotism.

The expansion of egotism

We have seen that egotism is *the* cause of evil in human beings. It is so deeply rooted within us that it cannot easily be overcome. We would be under the influence of a Luciferic illusion if we believed we could simply negate it, or easily defeat it. The laudable desire to become a better human being already reveals egotistical characteristics. Even when striving for good we cannot get beyond egotism. This is true of all striving to make progress and develop oneself spiritually, to tread a spiritual path. Egotism accompanies us more or less obviously or sometimes in a more subtle way.

Even in religious life, egotism plays a role. It is expressed in Luther's famous question, 'How do I find a merciful God?' and in the desire for one's own blessedness, which poisons genuine religious forces. Regret for sins committed in the past can lead to the crassest egotism. This happens when people want to have been better than they were; meanwhile they wallow in feelings of remorse and self-loathing experienced as an intensification of self-awareness. All self-pity is tainted deeply by egotism. Furthermore, when we actually do good we cannot avoid inflating our opinion of ourselves. We feel good about our deed and ourselves. The snake never sleeps. Unrecognized, it is present everywhere.

Is there any hope of escape? Or are we just too poisoned? There is indeed only one thing that will help. The moral demand that we 'fight egotism!' does not help. Neither does preaching 'Love thy neighbour,' which, by itself, usually just creates illusions.

What will help could be called, oddly enough, the *expansion* of egotism. This is the only way to gradually dissolve egotism and, step by step, to turn it to the service of good. This path consists in cultivating an active interest in everything that is not us, that surrounds us. If we attempt to *expand* our interest, which to begin with we have primarily for ourselves, to include as much as possible of the world around us then we can begin to breach the armour of egotism *from within*. The demand that we love our neighbour must be accompanied by an awakening of genuine interest in the world around us, in things both big and little. The first blow against egotism is struck when we are able to *understand* and above all to *experience* the world as permeated by spirit and therefore meaningful.

The significance of a spiritual view of the world cannot be overestimated. It can awaken an enduring interest in the phenomenon of the world because it speaks in detail of the meaningful connections and relationships present everywhere. This is what can motivate our devotion to the world: knowledge of the deeper relationships connecting everything. The simple moral imperative: 'turn to the world!' will ultimately prove itself to be fruitless.

Furthermore, the higher 'I' of the human being does not live 'for itself.' It knows that it signifies nothing for itself alone but much for the world. This characteristic of the higher 'I' is the absolute opposite of the Luciferic impulse, which wants to make our lower 'I', our old Adam, contract into itself and be sufficient unto itself. When we turn to the outside world with love and interest we 'imprint' the selfless gesture of our higher self into our lower self, thereby infusing it with the power of the new Adam.

Much can be done already in childhood to help or hinder a growing child in this regard. All education is extremely important in this area — home, school, and later, self-education. For good reason Waldorf School pedagogy has become very popular because it gives children a lively relationship to the world surrounding them. The relationship to the world the child naturally brings to school is not killed by one-sided materialism. The children are rather exposed to a way of seeing the world that is permeated with life and spirit. This is possible because of the worldview that inspired the curriculum and because the teachers are imbued with the same spiritually-based worldview. This creates a predisposition for the ability to turn with interest to the world in a healthy way in later life.

A dependency on sexual drives in later life is often partly caused by a materialistic and exclusively intellectual education in childhood. An education that teaches children to feel the beauty and majesty of the world in the ninth and tenth years of life works against such dependency because it calls for the healthy forces in us to unite with the world, and prevents us from sinking too deeply into our own bodily instincts. What has been properly instilled in the child continues working throughout life in a healthy way.

Everything that conveys the picture of an illusory reality is, fundamentally speaking, poison for humans, especially children. Film and television show a world that is false *in this form*. We do not mean to impugn the relative justification for these institutions. To be sure, they only foster interest in the world only in a very limited way; usually they undermine such interest by creating the illusion of satisfying our desire to know the world. From film and TV we gather pictures that convey perhaps accurate *reproductions of reality* but they are essentially abstractions, empty of concrete reality. As a remedy we can mention the practice of handcrafts or any activity involving craftsmanship; the arts such as music actually played, sung or composed; and sculpture, drawing or painting; in effect anything that leads to an experience of the beautiful and the majestic in the world, and education that stimulates this experience.

What has been planted in children's hearts through a proper education must be retrieved and consciously reawakened later in life through self-education, and a genuine interest in everything surrounding them. This can begin with the plant on the windowsill and extend to include every area of life. Preoccupation with oneself plays into the hand of egotism while loving attention to the world works against it. The world is healing for us.

Interest in the world includes interest in other humans, but it means an interest that asks, 'How does the other person feel about the world, how does he or she feel about me?' and not 'how do I feel about the other person?' The self will be all the stronger, not for the people it repels or rules over, but for the number of people it can include and carry. Strengthening the 'I' leads to a loving interest in, understanding of and compassion for, other people and their destinies.

This is especially true if we bear in mind the idea of repeated earth lives and the laws of destiny. For then I must say to myself it is not an accident that I happen to have met these people in my life, but it is determined by destiny in order for me to awaken and grow stronger through everything that gives me joy and suffering.

Against this background human encounters, friendships and marriage destinies lose their banal worldliness and the common task, the joint responsibility can be revealed even in the struggle for community. Awareness of this spiritual background to all human encounters encourages us not simply to avoid difficulties in human relationships, but not to meet them with simple aggression (for we ourselves, far in the past, might have been the deeper cause of such problems), but to understand them and have compassion, and — if the problems cannot be solved — to suffer and endure.

Of course, this will not immediately finish off egotism but the seed for its overcoming will have been planted. My interest in the plant in the window, in my garden can still be egotistical and burdened by too much self-awareness (pride, etc.). Nevertheless, I will have learned to look away from myself for moments and to make part of the world 'my concern.' This is what mothers and fathers do for their family. Their personal egotism expands to include children, parents etc. This path can lead us very far. What begins in a narrower circle can and should expand beyond the family. A healthy family has the wonderful possibility of also carrying other people, unfolding a healing atmosphere that gives others a space to live in. In this way 'family egotism' acquires something that extends beyond itself.

But egotism can still be expanded into even larger communities. This occurs when we make the goals of groups based on ideals our concern, our own goals. The more strongly such goals are directed to the spiritual, the less they will still be afflicted by egotism.

From this point of view we can also understand the significance of life in religious communities or communities with spiritual ideals. The further I ultimately expand my loving interest in the world, the less my personal, parochial egotism comes into play. The more I make the affairs of the world my affairs out of loving interest, the fewer things I have to encounter with antipathy, in an egotistical way. We admire people who have 'a lot of the world' within them. Today everyone can acquire something of this. In the future we will increasingly be able to slowly transform egotism from within, not extinguish it, thereby making it into a justified element within the world.

An attitude of soul that is particularly effective in working against Luciferic inclinations is Love of Duty. It is doubtless a difficult task not to feel that our daily duties are oppressive and confining, a necessary evil. Nevertheless, learning to love them is an essential step to overcoming egotism. Perhaps at first it will only be possible to love some of our everyday duties. This will be easiest if we are interested in them: interest in the people we must deal with, interest in the materials we must deal with, or if we remember the significance of our work, how other people are dependent upon it, or how, because of the income, it makes a meaningful life possible for our children, relatives or others for whom we are responsible.

We need to bear in mind that our higher self has an entirely different way of evaluating what we are achieving here on earth. It is aware of the far-reaching significance of our actions on earth. It knows that even the tiniest thing done in our everyday lives with loving devotion is not lost. It becomes a positive force that continues working and benefiting the whole world.

Exercises and learning

The next step is for us to realize that an interest in the world also includes an active interest in the spiritual world. When we activate this interest we are ready to learn and to practise, to do exercises. The ability to learn from experience is one of the highest capabilities we possess. In a very limited form we also find it in the training of animals. In humans, however, this ability exceeds the merely natural capacity for learning how to walk, speak, think and acquiring the traditional contents of education. It also includes the ability to summarize all the experiences of life in our consciousness. We are able to learn not only from positive experiences but especially from difficult and painful experiences, even those that create guilt. Even in the deepest abyss, the ability to learn can give us the prospect of return and restoration.

When we learn from our experiences we acquire knowledge. When this knowledge is combined with kindness of heart, it can evolve into wisdom. Kind-heartedness is most readily awakened through loving interest in other people. Two soul-forces are at work in wisdom: loving interest and the ability to learn. Wisdom and loving kindness are assuredly soul-forces of the new Adam.

Those who wish to work towards overcoming evil in the world and in themselves will one day decide to strengthen their ability to learn through conscious practice. Fundamentally speaking, everything we add to our lives voluntarily, by way of spiritual exercises, is of enormous importance; for it can strengthen and heal the power of the 'I.'

Nevertheless, there are some exercises that are not appropriate for everyone today. At least for Europeans and people with a western constitution a certain form of occultism can be very dangerous. Everything having to do with 'awakening the Kundalini force' is of this nature. Furthermore, most yoga exercises (breathing exercises and bodily positions) when employed as part of a path to higher knowledge are not to be recommended, although as part of a physical exercise programme they may be quite useful. This is connected with the fact that these exercises and meditations were developed in Asia at a time before the human 'I' became fully active in the earthly realm. These meditations do not take the human 'I' into account in the same sense that we are speaking of here: that the human 'I' has a task on earth. As a consequence, such meditations often lead to a weakening or damaging of the human self.

This is also true for the newer Eastern spiritual paths; they also are based on ancient Asian impulses without taking into account the evolution of the human self — at least the development of the self that has taken place in the West. A more exacting study of these spiritual paths shows this to be the case even when they advertise themselves as modern (e.g. Transcendental Meditation, Bhagwan, Ananda Marga, etc.). This is also true for the exercises that appear in Scientology, which have a more Ahrimanic nuance while Eastern paths tend to be more Luciferic.

Such judgments could easily appear to be dogmatic and partisan. I am well aware of that possibility. Nevertheless, it is not right to discuss occult exercises and meditations today without mentioning the danger of such meditations. Every genuine exercise and meditation of this kind has an effect. One must reckon with this. I feel called upon to point out these dangers because I have counselled many people who have been struggling with the serious effects of these particular meditative paths. It must also be stated that Anthroposophical meditations — thoughtlessly begun — can also have serious consequences. People often overlook the significance Rudolf Steiner attributed to proper preparation and preliminary exercises that should precede real meditation. However, many people today tend to begin occult exercises and meditations completely unprepared. Either there is insufficient endurance and consistency so that the meditative efforts amount to nothing, or else the necessary intensity is generated but due to inadequate preparation, one-sided effects cannot be avoided. It is always very problematic when meditative exercises are begun — of whatever kind — without good preparation.

One excellent preparation is the look-back-at-the-day exercise. In this exercise one looks back and remembers the events of the day in reverse order. It reinforces what we have said about learning. Looking back at the past day we practise a calm viewing of our experiences. Since the exercise is done backwards — from evening to morning — a special effort of will is associated with it, and therefore, when regularly practised, it leads to a strengthening of the will and the 'I.'

A necessary condition for proper meditation is to carry it out faithfully and consistently. At first this may appear obvious, but it proves to be extraordinarily difficult. Often, meditation, once begun, soon loses the attractive glow of something new. The egotism that may have been at work in the original impulse fades, but this fading creates an opportunity. Now the exercise can really be taken up in freedom! For neither from without nor from within is there a force that could compel me to meditate; on the contrary, our soul's own indolence provides the necessary opposition that needs to be overcome every time.

In this way, such exercises and meditations become truly voluntary deeds. Perhaps they are the only actions in the course of the day that are truly voluntary. It is this that gives them their enormous significance and thereby strengthens the self.

Additional preliminary exercises are necessary for those who wish to take up meditation in a serious way. Advice in such matters is available in the relevant literature.[4] This important realm of human activity is able to foster our inner growth. Of course, it does not protect us from evil, but it does contribute to building the new Adam, the tender shoot of a new being within us. By means of meditation higher spiritual forces are drawn down into our earthly realm.

Not everyone will immediately want to take up meditation and occult exercises. Nevertheless, the element of mental exercise and the practice of certain inner soul faculties is important for everyone today. There are many different ways to exercise the soul, to exercise our senses, in such a way that we strengthen our soul as well as our 'self' in the morning and the evening. What can be said from the point of view of religion will be the content of the next chapter.

The significance of art

Another area where we can practise active interest in the world is in the realm of art. For art — and we mean here active participation in creating art — can only be created through actively turning to the world with loving interest. Indeed, all creative activity is important for the same reasons. In various ways Erich Fromm has pointed out that creativity is able to compensate for evil. In view of the desire for violent revenge that can sometimes arise within the soul, he says,

> A human being who lives a productive life does not have this need or hardly at all. Even if he has been injured, offended or wounded, he forgets through the productivity of his life, what was done to him in the past. His capacity to create proves to be stronger than his desire for revenge.[5]

Waldorf pedagogy puts great value on artistic and crafts activities through all the grades for just this reason. In the future, a life in artistic and handwork crafts will be extraordinarily important for people. The possibilities for adults are greatly expanded through anthroposophy: eurythmy and speech formation, for example, can be done by people even into old age, also as therapeutic exercises.

In the space available, it is not possible to go into the different kinds of art and their various effects on the human being. Music, painting, sculpture, writing, etc., handwork too, all offer a wealth of opportunities for every kind of person regardless of what their gifts or situation may be. It can be demonstrated how any specific form of artistic activity affects a specific member (physical, etheric, astral or 'I') of the human constitution in working to harmonize and heal. The creative forces that have been instilled in humans are not developed at all in our civilization. They lie fallow in the soul but are yearning for expression. They are present in everyone and want to be brought to bear in the world around us. Modern occupations and careers, as they have developed, allow no space or time for such activity. And what passes for leisure time activities only contribute to paralysing or blocking these artistic forces.

There are two possible consequences:
— These artistic forces break out in disruptive ways, in crime, aggression and vandalism. They threaten to become the negative characteristic of our time. (One thinks of the excesses at sporting events or of sexual excess.)
— The paralysing of will-forces: this creates humans who can only consume because the creative capacities in their souls are inaccessible to them.

In these two tendencies we again see the Luciferic and Ahrimanic extremes. Creative artistic activity works against those extremes. Those who can repeatedly immerse themselves in creative activity have a better chance of being alive, flexible and creative, also in their thinking, their social interactions and human relationships. We are speaking here of the healing possibilities of art which can be so helpful for those whose daily work requires them to engage soul-forces that not creative.

It is the 'I' that stirs into motion in art. In this movement it discovers that it does not have to egotistically close itself up but that it can go into the world actively bringing forth something new. This is the therapeutic and joyous experience in all artistic activity. Practising art signifies a great deal more than is contained in the moment of practice. It means that the human 'I' can sense something of what lies behind the doors of paradise, of what has been lost and must be found again.

The human ability to celebrate festivals is also connected to creativity. It threatens to disappear today. The community experience of meaningfully celebrated festivals can make a major contribution to the healing of evil. The great religious festivals will again acquire significance, though, of course only if they are understood as well as celebrated.[6] A strong social sense, a feeling of community, can be carried over from festivals into all of life. They contribute to the human ability to work from the 'I' into community with other people and the spiritual world. For in religious festivals two things come together: creative activity that gives form to community, and the elevation of our souls to the worlds, with which our higher self is connected.

The helping presence of Christ

Many people today are alienated from religious life. The fact that religion in the past has so often been driven by egotism no doubt contributes to this. All too easily the practice of religion becomes a striving for 'eternal blessedness' and/or wallowing in unhealthy feelings.

The Christian Community, and the religious life it cultivates, seeks to counter this danger through an increased interest in the world, with the help of knowledge concerning spiritual realms, which until now seemed to be accessible only to faith. The fact that faith can again be supported and illuminated by knowledge gives the 'I' of individual human beings a sure footing in life. Concerning the most essential aspects of life we are not thrown back on a faith that still appears questionable and based on a childish relationship to God.[7] Today our relationship to God should be based on the full consciousness of the 'I,' of the human self. We are spiritually autonomous beings who have come of age. This holds true in the celebration of sacramental acts where the conscious participation of all who are present is expected.[8]

Prayer

Given the circumstances described in the previous paragraph, the religious life can make an essential contribution to strengthening the 'I' and overcoming evil. To begin with, we have the prayer of individuals. Yet prayer itself can easily become egotistical. On the other hand, the fact that there is no 'I' or 'me' in the Lord's Prayer only 'us' and 'our' is especially effective in our efforts to avoid egotism. Anyone saying this prayer cannot possibly say it only for himself but must always include at least one or more other people.

Prayer is an immediate and direct turning to the spiritual world, an immediate speaking to God. One says 'you' directly to another. Combined with this 'you' is devotion and reverence, our highest and purest soul-forces, which are able to lead us beyond ourselves. For just as we can sink below our own level, so too we can lift ourselves beyond ourselves. Then it is possible for higher spiritual forces to shine into our souls, forces that are unable to shine into us, indeed are not permitted to stream into us until we have opened ourselves to them through our own efforts.

With the Fall into sin, Lucifer grabbed the soul-forces of man for himself. He is still doing this today, which makes us unfree. Lucifer became the adversary of freedom. Although he brought freedom to humans he brought it as freedom from the spiritual world but not from himself. Only when we have also freed ourselves from Lucifer (and Ahriman) will we have broken through to the full freedom of 'sons of God' as we read in Paul (Rom.8:21).

Herein we see the significance of every free, voluntary action: it represents a step forward on this path. Meditation as a voluntary deed is placed at the side of prayer as a turning to God. Meditation, too, can be answered by God. The spiritual world is not allowed to bring its higher forces to bear in human souls *out of its own initiative* — as Lucifer does — for then we would lose our freedom. However, when we freely turn to the spiritual world, to God, he can also answer us in freedom. Reverence and devotion are uplifting forces towards spirit. The 'I' can upright itself with them and thereby meet the world of its origin. Every genuine prayer strengthens the 'I', battles evil, builds the inner, future human being.

We can go a step further. We indicated above that in sleep, human beings, with their 'I', are lifted up into a higher world. It is not unreasonable to think that entrance into this higher world is intimately influenced by what a person allows to pass through their souls in terms of feelings, thoughts and moods during the day. We can think of oil spills and of marine birds, whose wings are covered with oil and therefore unfit for flying; they cannot lift themselves up. The soul's power to lift itself into higher realms during sleep depends upon the soul's 'feathered wings' being clean. Evening prayer — and with evening prayer we always mean the Lord's Prayer — gives us the power of flight for a proper entrance into the spiritual world during sleep.

Something similar then holds true for morning prayer. The experiences in the spiritual world that we bring with us out of sleep, though deep in our unconscious, are expressed in the moods we live with during the day. We can bring something like a 'dew' from the spirit that rests on the 'meadows of the soul.' To surrender ourselves immediately to the everyday concerns of life means we lose what could otherwise continue working through the day. Prayer in the morning absorbs something of the spiritual forces of the night and carries them into the day.

What we are pointing to here means a great deal more for the moods, tensions and feelings of dissatisfaction that accompany us in everyday life than one might at first think. For anyone unable to lift himself up to the spiritual world at night, where he can converse with his higher self, will find it very difficult to be well balanced the next day. He will carry his dissatisfaction with the night within his soul, where it can become a source of evil. Much evil could be avoided if humans could find in sleep, not only a counterbalance for their depleted life-forces, but also for their spiritual forces.

Christ's presence in ritual

There is much that could be said about the meaning of the renewed ritual as practised in the Christian Community. We will speak of only one aspect here: the forces of devotion and reverence in ritual that lead to an encounter with the spiritual world, not on the other side of the threshold of earthly consciousness as in sleep, but within the earthly. For this reason true rituals have such an extraordinary significance for humans, because they make the spiritual present in the earthly realm.

Of course, it is true that God is present in all places and at all times. Christ said, 'Behold, I am with you always, even unto the end of earthly time' (Matt.28:20). These words point to the eternal closeness of the divine. Johannes Tauler was the man who said that God is always with us but we are not always with him. Through ritual we can 'come to God.' We approach God by elevating our soul-forces in rituals.

But it is also true that he approaches us to bring about a deeper presence. Perhaps the following picture will aid understanding. The light from the sun is always present; its light is at work on the earth as soon as it rises over the horizon. Yet it is also possible to concentrate the rays of the sun with a lens, making the sun's light incomparably more powerful.

Christians have been aware since ancient time that in cultic forms of religious services, the human soul is elevated to experience the presence of Christ. Furthermore, ritual makes it possible to intensify one's experience of Christ's presence — just as the sun's rays can be concentrated. The celebration of the sacrament carries the presence of Christ and with him a measure of the spiritual world into the earthly. But our higher 'I' lives in the spiritual world. With our experience of Christ in ritual we can also experience that something of our higher 'I' comes to meet us with him, that Christ brings us our higher self. We can feel that in our celebration of the Christian sacraments we become more truly 'ourselves.' This finds expression in the name given to the religious service, i.e., the Eucharist or Mass, in the Christian Community: The Act of Consecration of Man.

When this service is carried out, it is protected by itself from our egotism. In the long run it will lead only to the aforementioned experiences if it is celebrated with reverence and devotion. Those who only come seeking something for themselves will soon leave. Only those who learn to disregard themselves, lift up their souls in devotion and offer their soul-forces to God, can experience how again and again their higher self is ignited and united with their 'everyday self.' They 'draw' Christ to themselves (as Paul says) and 'put on the new Adam,' in the sense that something of the new human being becomes reality in us.

It is not merely a pious symbol to say that Christian culture reaches its peak in Communion. Taking bread and wine as the body and blood of Christ points to the reality of which we are speaking. Of course, this reality can assume varying degrees of intensity according to the degree of devotion, but it *is* present — just as the sun is present during the day, even if often hidden behind a cloud.

What we experience unconsciously in sleep is brought to our earthly consciousness in ritual. What takes place in sleep outside our body begins to become a reality even into our body and blood, indeed, in such a way that we ourselves participate much more strongly than in sleep.

Christ and the human 'I'

Our higher 'I' comes close to us with Christ who brings it to us, so to speak. Our 'better self' lives in Christ. In turning to Christ, I am not striving towards a being who is entirely different from me. I am reaching out for the highest ideal that can possibly live within me, my very own true being. We could also say that the highest picture of what I can be is already a full reality in Christ. In Christ, this reality comes to meet me so that I can say: 'Not I, but Christ in me,' and I do not mean some kind of channelling or possession by another being, but rather the highest fulfilment of my true being. In order to grasp this fact more deeply we can think of a crystal, perhaps a golden topaz, that can only display its full brilliance in the sunlight, not in shadow or darkness. The crystal loses nothing of itself when the sun shines through it — on the contrary, only then does it reveal all of its beauty. Thus we only come fully to ourselves through Christ without in the least having to lose ourselves. The human being only achieves his highest fulfilment through the ability to give Christ a space within.

This is all possible because Christ himself became a human being. He brought his existence close to human existence in a decisive deed. Furthermore, he not only 'took on' human existence, he actually transformed it and lifted it up to a higher level of being, freed from the sickness of sin. This is basically what the Gospels are speaking about. In their pictures and words describing the Transfiguration, the Resurrection, and Ascension we see the stages of this basic fact.

We can decipher these pictures of Christ's life if we consider that the effect of the Fall into sin in the members of Jesus (physical, etheric, and astral bodies) were 'undone.' By dwelling in the physical, life and soul bodies of a human being it was possible for Christ to expel the Adversaries from these members and thereby to heal completely 'the sickness of sin' within the bodily nature of Jesus.

Already in the Transfiguration (Matt.17) the bodily nature of Christ Jesus began to shine like the sun for the vision of the disciples, announcing the spiritualization of the body. When Christ then went through death and resurrection he was able to tear the physical body away from Ahriman. The bodily nature of the Resurrected one was then fully spiritualized.

Christ stands before us as the one who has become 'man' in the highest sense of the word: the *new* Adam. Not only can we see our higher self protected in him, we can also feel him as the one who carries for us the 'purely human,' that is 'purified humanness,' that he created by overcoming the Fall. Ever since Christ walked on the earth as a human being, the essence of our humanity is lifted up and preserved in Christ; and we can draw it close when we 'attract' Christ.

These Pauline expressions are much more real than we are generally prepared to believe. We speak of turning to Christ as a source of healing. We are intentionally avoiding the use of the word 'faith.' What we mean by the word 'turning' is very simple: using the Gospels, understood with the help of anthroposophy, to form a picture of Christ, of the resurrected Christ. Then thinking of him, imagining what his presence would feel like, feeling his deep connection with us, sensing his love, wanting to love him, seeking to understand him ... His power becomes active in us when we turn to him. If being in the presence of a good person already makes us a little better ourselves because some of his or her goodness flows over to us, then how much more can flow to us from the presence of Christ.

For those who live in prayer and ritual all of this can gradually and increasingly become a profound reality and an affair of the heart. Our life gradually receives another dimension, our 'I' gets a new orientation — not that all evil thereby melts away from us. Perhaps the opposite occurs: that we have greater difficulties than before and are exposed to greater trials. This phenomenon can be observed in the destiny of the disciples. Something else is also present because the effects of Christ's presence extends not only to the 'I' and the soul but also into the life-forces and the body. Just as the effects of the Fall into sin reached all the way through the soul into the physical body, so too the healing of the sickness of sin extends all the way into the whole human being. Paul was pointing to this fact when he said, 'Therefore, if anyone is in Christ he is a new creation' (2Cor.5:17 JM) Something of the future human being, the new Adam, lives in us — perhaps at first as only a faint breath — when we seek Christ in our own lives.

Thankfulness, trust instead of worry and fear

We have yet to deal with worry and fear. These sit even deeper in the human soul and are even more difficult to overcome than egotism.

Above and beyond what we have already said, there are three forces in the soul that work to overcome fear: thankfulness, trust and devotion to life.

Thankfulness and trust can be connected to prayer in a special way. In the evening we can develop a mood of prayer out of our gratitude. Our 'I' matures to a new strength when we can thank God not only for the beautiful things that come to us in the course of a day, but also for the difficult, even painful events. Practising gratitude is something that begins to raise us above egotism. It connects us in a very special way with the spiritual world and our higher 'I' when we bring our gratitude for all of our destiny, the joyful and the painful events of the day, to Christ who guides our destiny.

In the morning, something similar holds for trust: it carries the mood of prayer for the start of the day. Just as we unite with our higher self in gratitude because gratitude for our destiny lives in our higher self, so too with the trust that whatever may come, it is being brought to us through the wisdom of our destiny, through Christ. For worry and fear do not live in our higher self but, rather a trust that knows Christ as the guide of human destiny.

As we cultivate gratitude in the evening as a foundation for an atmosphere of prayer we will increasingly be able to feel that, basically, we can grow and learn from anything and everything that meets us in the course of the day — and therefore we can be grateful for everything. This will make it more and more possible to enliven our experience of the other mood at the start of the day: whatever may come to me today I trust that I can grow and learn from it. Such trust based on experience and united with Christ can grow even into love for what the day may bring us (even love for the daily, perhaps difficult, duties that life imposes on us). Such love is a tremendous aid in our battle against the deeply-rooted fear of what may come.

It is not possible to change ourselves in this regard overnight. It takes time. On the other hand, it is clear how much aggression, suffering, even evil comes into human relationships because of fear. One usually fears the apparent superiority of the other and then, because of this fear, becomes aggressive oneself. Much aggression is ultimately the result of weakness and fear.

Jacques Lusseyran, who was blinded as a child and then broke through to an 'inner seeing' describes in his autobiography the nature of this inner perception.[9] He speaks of an 'inner light' that does not give him any perception in the usual, external sense but makes possible a perception of something that reveals to him the essence of a landscape, of a person, etc. In this way he could recognize with much greater certainty than others the quality and the attitude of a person. However, this 'inner light' dimmed immediately as soon as a negative mood entered his soul, like fear, anger, impatience, malice. 'Still there were times during which the light dimmed and almost disappeared. That was always the case when I was fearful ... What the loss of my eyesight could not do, fear could do: it made me blind.'

We see here the profound effect of the Ahrimanic influence on the soul. What Lusseyran experienced is basically true for everyone: fear makes us blind, even blind to the good, to the right step that could lead us or others forward. What Saint-Exupéry said in *The Little Prince* is true, 'It is only with the heart that one can see rightly.' However, the heart cannot see well when it is ruled by fear.

And the opposite is also true: if we can attain a trust in the future and all that it may bring to us, whatever it may be, then this trust will work like a light illuminating the opportunities that are coming towards us. If we are able to approach other people calmly with an open heart, without fear or the aggression that derives from fear, without impatience or malice then, through this fact alone enormous good can flow into us and the world.

The gradual overcoming of fear is ultimately connected with the creation of the new Adam; there is no fear in him because he is created out of the eternal forces in us. Learning to feel eternal forces within us means learning how to trust. In many ways it is a very long path, nevertheless, it *is* a path.

Thankfulness, trust and the third attitude: devotion to the duties of life. Love of duty comes to us here from a different perspective. Precisely those who seek to lead a religious life (or a spiritual life in general) do well to conscientiously fulfill their daily obligations as something that they want to do to fulfill their destiny, their karma. Saying 'yes' to the life task that we have to take up, 'yes' to the life situation we find ourselves in, and showing loving devotion to our daily actions releases strong forces for healing and overcoming the sickness of sin.

Let us look back at the previously mentioned motifs. Regarding egotism we have:
— Motivation for working towards good provided by a spiritual world-view.
— The 'expansion' of egotism and its overcoming 'from within.'

— Love of duty.
— Strengthening the 'I' and the 'new Adam.'
— Learning and practising verses, meditation and prayer.
— Practising art as a form of active interest in the world.
— Experiencing meaningful festivals as an element in healing evil.

In this chapter, regarding fear, we have added:
— Prayer and the celebration of rituals such as the Mass.
— Experiencing the significance of Christ's activity for the 'I.'
— Thankfulness and trust.
— Devotion to life and the tasks it imposes upon us.

Our true (not our imagined) relationship to the divine world and to Christ plays a decisive role in our struggle with evil. Good comes to meet us in Christ in its most essential form. He can become our brother and helper in the struggle with evil as well as our leader on all paths of destiny.

CHAPTER 11

Transformation through Destiny

Our destiny is not a series of accidents, at least not the essential events. It fits into a series of earth lives in a meaningful way. Our destiny works with a certain inevitability in everything that meets us from outside (misfortune, etc.), and in the people we meet. How we then react and what we make of these encounters is entirely up to us.

On the other hand we *can* 'wander away' from our destiny. Then it is a matter for the guide of our destiny, our guardian angel, to confront us with the experiences necessarily to our karma. Our destiny has access to a very large band-width of possibilities and can even allow false, illusory paths, wrong ways and byways as well as detours (it is not a one-way street). The guiding spirits of destiny must, at times, become extraordinarily inventive. Hence, it can be said that no essential event in destiny — to the extent that it comes from outside — is an accident, and that no one can escape his destiny. What is important here is a fundamental mood of soul that feels, 'my destiny is in agreement with my own higher self, therefore, at the deepest level it represents nothing foreign to me.' Our destiny is meaningful, firstly, because opportunities arise for us to compensate for injustices we ourselves have committed, or that were committed against us, and, secondly, because this balance can be arranged so that it fosters the development of *everyone* involved. The ancient law of karma, 'an eye for an eye, and a tooth for a tooth,' which was appropriate for an earlier age, has been transformed by Christ. Destiny today is still effective in bringing about an exacting balance for all injustice and guilt, but no longer in the sense of punishment that revenges like with like, but rather in a way that creates wakefulness and strength in the place where weakness caused injustice.

Humans have the ability to learn. Destiny is the teacher although the actual learning occurs in large measure after death. We rise into the spiritual world after death. Just as before birth we have a preview, so too after death we have a 'post view' of our earthly life. Then all our mistakes and weaknesses, all the injustice in our actions lie unveiled before us in all clarity. We learn to recognize the grip the Adversaries have on us. The desire arises in our will to do better and make up for all the wrongs we have committed, both sins of commission and of omission. This desire leads to the formation (in detail) of destiny for our next life on earth.

Rudolf Steiner reports that for a time after death we are in a special part of the spiritual world where we experience all that our actions have ever caused another person to feel. We feel the joy and pain that we have caused others. This profound experience has extraordinarily far-reaching consequences and is accompanied by a great deal of pain. However, we seek such experiences after death, despite the suffering associated with them because they give us self-knowledge at a depth not possible in our earthly existence.

The 'I' and the soul of a human being are, in this way, intense learners. And they carry what they have learned into their next life on earth. The inclination to push through with one's own selfish goals, ignoring the injustice done to others, becomes a little less elemental. 'Nobler' people live more intensely than others with an unconscious memory of self-knowledge acquired after death. Conscience also has its roots in such experiences. Of course, conscience can be deformed in many regards and filled with false orientations. Freud and others are to a certain extent right about such possibilities. However, the actual kernel, the ability to create a conscience, is connected with the processes described above. Conscience is the voice in us, which — as long as it has not been distorted and alienated — 'remembers' the experiences that came to us as a result of the injustices we committed in the past.

Extreme destinies: criminality and suicide

Now it may appear as though human beings progress continually upward on their spiritual path as a consequence of what was described in the last section. However, as life shows us, that is certainly not the case. We can see countless human beings who seem to have 'bottomed out' in life — often without there being any way to bring them real help — and we must admit that we ourselves might be in their place were it not for more favourable conditions at the start of our own lives.

In light of such questions we must once again remember that destiny does not proceed in a sentimental way. Pointing this out does not mean a lack of compassion. Life produces many lives on the edge of existence. Could the reason for this be that even lives such as these nevertheless present a possibility for learning, perhaps precisely because of their extremity?

These extreme destinies show that destiny grants us a wide field of action, even the 'right' to make wrong decisions. For only what comes to us from without is to a certain extent 'determined.' Predestination is much less at work in our decisions. In this realm today the 'I,' the human self, must take a stand with its yes or no.

In the course of an earthly life, most people are led at least once into an incredibly difficult situation in order to experience the deepest forces called forth within them. Every human being must come to know something of earth's depths; above all, strong souls often do not hesitate to seek out such destinies. They have the strength to be deeply immersed in dark situations and to learn from them. The history of saints is full of descriptions of how a destiny deeply involved with darkness experiences a sharp turn to good.

Certainly this turning does not usually occur in one lifetime, sometimes only after several earth lives. And it does not take place by itself; it is not automatic. The necessity to experience the darkness of earth also presents an opportunity to become entangled in the darkness. These circumstances can result in destinies which, according to a conventional middle class point of view, should not have been allowed and appear to be completely permeated by evil. Not even the most capable and courageous mountain climber is safe from a fall. Such earth lives can only make sense when seen with a perspective that includes future earth lives.

Furthermore, the powerful forces required to master life can later be generated precisely out of such destinies. People who stand in life with certainty and strength so great that they can sometimes give direction to entire communities, did not acquire their strength through previous lifetimes filled with nothing but serenity and happiness. Of course, such considerations must not lead us to conclude that people should be allowed to do the worst. Those who wantonly unite themselves with evil are preparing a severe destiny for themselves, from which they can perhaps only be saved by others. This is summarized in the words of Rudolf Steiner:

The soul must never want to fall into the abyss.
Nevertheless, it must acquire wisdom from the Fall (Fourth
Mystery Drama, 6th Scene).

Another aspect must be mentioned here: like everything else in the world, the conviction of the truth of repeated earth lives also has a dark side. It was not without reason that for two thousand years Christianity stressed the uniqueness of one life on earth. For in a certain sense every earth life is truly unique: firstly, because the particular circumstances of history cannot be repeated. An incarnation in ancient Egypt, in ancient Greece is unrepeatable in its uniqueness. Secondly, it must also be said that what is left undone today at its proper time, can only be made up for tomorrow in pain. Anyone who decided to live a lazy life because of opportunities available in a future lifetime would have to do hard penance for this negligence. 'What you can do today must not be put off till tomorrow.' These words are of the utmost importance in this regard. For tomorrow can bring needs, for which we must prepare today. Without the results of that preparation we will stand empty-handed, unable to act or perhaps even to perceive the need. We will have let ourselves down and most probably many others as well. It will be painful.

When properly understood, the truth of repeated earth lives can only be an incentive for responsibility, not for indolence. It creates a moral sense of responsibility for our fellow human beings. To deny compassion and help for other people because they are suffering from their 'own karma and self-inflicted destiny' is unjust and would make us guilty. A proper understanding of how destiny works can only lead us to do all that we can to help and support others.

One of the most tragic events in destiny is suicide. Not only does it create severe consequences in the life after death that immediately follows; actually it can never lead to what was intended. It is not possible to extinguish one's own being, and the destiny that leads into a new life on earth will necessarily have to bring forth the same old difficulties in a different form. However, it must also be said that today, as tragic as it is in every instance when someone takes his or her own life, we are frequently not dealing with a true suicide. The consciousness that leads to the deed can already be so reduced, changed and darkened that the individual cannot be held fully responsible. In which case, the severe consequences indicated will not necessarily ensue.

It is clear that the idea of reincarnation with the concomitant formation of destiny or karma can cast much light on the riddles of destiny. Yet we must add this: confronted with the deepest questions of destiny — criminality and suicide — there is nevertheless something that eludes explanation. This is where the question of destiny really becomes the question of evil. These questions are connected to the riddle of the individual human personality itself, and this riddle of the individual human being cannot be fully fathomed because every human being in his or her decisions represents a mystery, which, for our present day consciousness, can only be experienced but not fully understood. Human suffering always represents a cry for help not for judgment.

Furthermore, we should bear in mind that 'karmic laws,' do not by themselves call forth something good. Individual human beings must themselves want good and choose it out of their own innermost personal desire. Events of destiny can present us with chances and perhaps even give us a nudge but it is the individual alone who takes hold of them or lets the opportunity slip by. Good does not 'automatically' arise through destiny over the course of several earth lives. It is created only by human beings — today more than ever.

Freedom and responsibility

Another profound question for which we have no final solution, but perhaps a new perspective is the question of freedom and responsibility in human actions. We have already considered this question using the examples of terrorists and Robespierre: guilty or not guilty? Responsible or not? Free or driven by certain motivations?

This question can be seen from the perspective of all-inclusive laws of destiny governing all lives on earth. For in their lives after death these perpetrators will definitely become fully conscious of the horror of their deeds. Then they will *want* to take on the karmic consequences of their actions. Presumably they will be much in need of help but perhaps also very much inclined to good.

However, there are also lives that bear not only personal karma but are also marked by the destiny of an age. In lives of this kind the human soul experiences a destiny necessitated not so much by individual karma but rather by the destiny of humanity at the time and place of his or her incarnation. Such destinies can be seen as 'characteristic' or 'representative.' Something that concerns all of humanity but cannot and should not be experienced by every individual human being becomes visible in such lives.

The karmic effects of such destinies must certainly be evaluated differently. Before we spoke of the subsequent need for help in a future incarnation for certain people. Help will definitely come to such people because what they did was part of the 'karma of mankind.' So help will be available to them as members of the human race when it is time to deal with the debt of guilt they incurred.

The general rule must apply, however, that a person's deeds are taken seriously, otherwise the spiritual world would not be taking seriously the human beings who were affected by that person's deeds. A child that reaches into a fire burns himself — he experiences the immediate consequences of his deed and will certainly not repeat it. Experiences cannot be replaced by admonitions and commandments; they have a fundamental character. The child learns immediately that there are things on earth that one should be very careful with. This experience can be transferred to other things — it counts 'once and for all.' One does not have to test everything.

Something similar holds for the guilt we incur in destiny. Many experiences — even those of an abysmal sort — must be gone through so that strength can be built up to avoid them in the future. Through the experience of a burned finger, the child awakens fundamentally to a certain area of life; before the burn it was not yet awake and couldn't be. We only awaken to our responsibility through the experience of guilt. That we are still asleep in many of our actions, are not conscious of the full extent of their consequences and are therefore unfree, may still be true.[10] Destiny will still bring us the full consequences of our actions, just as the child is burned by fire even though he is ignorant and therefore innocent. In the same way we can awaken through our deeds. The intensified feeling of responsibility for life that some people have is connected with experiences in previous lives on earth. The entire destiny of mankind aims to lead us from an original innocence and unfree condition to guilt in order to bring us to freedom.

The fact that many people today are far from any feeling of independent responsibility is probably due to their not having any far-reaching individual experiences in destiny in their previous lives. It is possible that in earlier earth lives they still lived embedded in a group and therefore had little individual experience shaping their lives.

Their present incarnation is, for many people, the first opportunity for individual experience. Hence, the naiveté or even recklessness many contemporaries display in their behaviour.

We can see then that our destiny does not proceed out of freedom and responsibility — nor was it different with Adam — but rather leads in that direction. Naturally, this is not a straight path with a guaranteed ascent. In every lifetime we face new, unknown situations in which we can go astray and fail. For those who are 'advanced' in destiny the tasks and trials get more difficult; the higher we climb the deeper the abyss, the greater the danger. The words from Goethe's *Faust*, 'Man errs as long as he strives' points to this truth. But we can also take the other truth from *Faust*, which represents the only guarantee in our lives: genuine striving combined with love can expect help without which in the end we would not go far.

Raised for evil? The question of environmental influences

There is a widespread view that the causes of our behaviour in later life come into existence in childhood. The extent to which this might be the case is a subject that will never see an end of discussion.

Nevertheless, it is easy to see something justified in this view. Görres himself indicates that this view has limits: 'Not every frustration provokes aggression ... Based on my experience as a doctor I can say that even in an environment of dealers, thugs and whores an un-bribable conscience can arise.' And yet, it is also true that, 'the opinion that instinctive drives, if simply indulged, would somehow become harmonized by themselves, can only be held by someone who has not tested this theory against the various experiences of everyday life.' Hence, a limit must be set to the overflowing desires and needs of children.

From the point of view of reincarnation the childhood we experience, the environment in which we grow up, including the genetic inheritance we start life with, is not an accident. We must also remember that we show no sentimentality when choosing our destiny. In our pre-earthly existence, we are influenced neither by Luciferic temptations that would lead us to strive for maximum pleasure, nor by Ahrimanic darkness that would prevent us from recognizing the significance of pain and suffering for human spiritual evolution.

Is it an impossible thought that we ourselves — at least to a certain extent — have prepared the hindrances and difficulties from which we must later suffer? Isn't it the case that in every field of endeavour, in which we wish to become proficient, we must voluntarily undergo exhausting, perhaps even painful, training and face many difficulties in order to achieve our goal? The old cliché comes to mind: 'No pain, no gain.'

Our eternal self struggles, learns and matures in all the difficulties we must overcome or perhaps just endure. This is true even when it may at first appear that a human life has been so influenced by a horrific childhood that it is now unsalvageable. Even then, in the uniquely tailored difficulties created by that imprinting the spiritual kernel of the individual experiences a great deal, even if the spiritual self is at first unable to assert itself at all. It will carry the experiences, the defeats and rare victories as an inner stimulus and strength through death into the spiritual world, where they will be taken up by hierarchical beings and shaped into a new destiny that will carry the person further.

This is much more the case when we not only passively accept our destiny but actively wrestle (not argue!) with it, seeking to wring out the good to be found therein, even if we are prepared merely to endure the inevitable again and again. We think of the destinies of Kepler, Henry Stanley, Hellen Keller, Jacques Lusseyran — to name a few. Then forces arise that lead us forward as we have seen, for example, in the wisdom of fairy tales.

Consequently, we can regard much of what we have received from our parents, siblings, teachers, and the entire environment in which we are raised, as our destiny. We can accept it because we realize that it does not impact us blindly but we ourselves choose it, because it provides the material for us to make something out of ourselves.

Where debt arises — this is how the laws of destiny apply — it will be compensated. When people incur guilt and debt because of their behaviour towards others, as compensation the other can expect their help in a future earth life. And vice versa, when I acquire guilt and owe others, in the life between death and birth I will develop an innermost drive to compensate another person for this debt by doing good, and at the place where the guilt was incurred — on the earth. In this sense we should not think of our destiny as 'our' destiny but as one interwoven with giving and taking in the destinies of other people.

We are less concerned with the truth of theories concerning environmental influences in destiny than we are with the meaningful ways in which those influences weave into human destiny when they are seen in light of reincarnation.

The person next to me

Indebtedness between people can also lead to positive effects, namely to deeper relationships in destiny and the possibility of helping people. The interweaving of destinies has a double perspective: it can lead to mutual development and the elevation of both people to a higher level of being. It can lead to deep joy caused by the encounter with the other person that lasts throughout life. It can be an encounter that enriches our entire life. Often difficulties, dangers and indebtedness appear on one side.

The other side, however, consists of the genuine help that one person can give another. This is something purely human that only exists in the animal kingdom in a very incipient way. In the human realm 'helping out' exists on all stages of existence — beginning with help in being born. A mother, for example, gives life to another person from her body and then supports and cares for that person for many years. Teachers help their students. Doctors, nurses and caregivers help the sick and dying. In all these cases it is necessary for the caregiver to be devoted, to some extent, to the one who needs help. Such help is based on sacrifice.

Then there are the inner forms of help. We are much more deeply connected to the people in our 'circle of destiny' than we know. The thoughts, feelings and impulses that we send (even unconsciously) to other people have a real effect. Everybody can experience what happens if they surround a person whom they do not like with nothing but positive, loving thoughts: a change for the better in the relationship is inevitable. In this way we inwardly influence one another as strongly as we do externally.

Just the attempt to understand someone, to feel 'with' someone helps him. In this field there is every degree of intensity. One of the most intensive helps occurs when we forgive debt. We thereby transform a force in the soul that is negative. For example, grudges, the 'I can't take it anymore' attitude, and the desire for revenge, can be changed into good that then leads to further transformation. Forgiveness and petitionary prayer can be redemptive forces. This points to a higher kind of help, to the help that can come from Christ.

Redemption or self-redemption

Can man not save himself in the end? Is Christ's help really necessary?

In the expression 'self-redemption' we touch on an objection to the idea of reincarnation that is frequently brought forward and based on a presupposition. The redemptive deed of Christ is denied and made worthless when one asserts that human beings are in a position to save themselves by compensating for their sins in successive earth lives. It must be stressed that this is not the understanding of anthroposophy. It is correct to say that human beings must themselves achieve compensation for their own personal indebtedness. This portion must not be taken away from them for it provides an incentive for the inner path. The full seriousness of destiny that weighs upon us educates us to a full sense of responsibility. This is meant by Paul when he says: 'whatever a man sows, that he will also reap' (Gal.6:7 RSV) or also the words from Matthew 7:2, 'and the measure you give will be the measure you get.'

However, there is another realm affected by human sin. It is a realm where I cannot create compensation. If I cause bodily harm to another person — for example knock out an eye — I can seek to balance my karmic account with that person by compensating him in some way but I cannot replace the eye. The debt I have incurred has 'spilled over' into a realm of being in which I have no power, where, despite all the goodwill in the world, I cannot undo what I have done. This example shows us that there is an objective and a subjective aspect connected to every indebtedness.

This is true for failings in which the objective aspect is not so obvious. Since man is in no way an insignificant creation in the universe, but has far-reaching significance for the world, his mistakes and lapses also extend to deeper levels of being. Rudolf Steiner explained that a lie, for example, not only destroys the trust of other people, but also destroys something in the spiritual world. In our actions as moral agents we are most intimately connected with the spiritual forces in the world.

The Adversaries counted on these objective effects of human sinfulness in their attempt to cut mankind off from the spiritual world. The future destinies of human beings increasingly darkened. In this way, mankind would have had to lose all contact with the spirit. Perhaps one part of the guilt incurred during human destiny would have been compensated and balanced out. But the other objective part, which cannot be transformed by human beings, would have forced man into the abyss of evil.

Christ's arrival on earth, which surprised the Adversaries, interrupted this development. When Christ took the 'sins of the world' upon himself he could then roll away the stone that would have caused the earth to become mankind's grave. He took it upon himself to give what was necessary to dissolve the objective consequences of sin. From his own life-forces he brought forth compensation for all the life-forces destroyed by mankind. The picture of Christ on the cross is a representation of this fact of earth's evolution. In the Gospel story of the woman caught in adultery this truth is presented in archetypal form.

> And Jesus went to the Mount of Olives. But as soon as the next day dawned he was already in the Temple again, and the people flocked to him, and he sat down and taught them. Then the scribes and the Pharisees brought a woman who had been caught in adultery, and they placed her in the middle. Then they said to him, 'Master, this woman has been caught in the act of adultery. In the Law, Moses commands us to stone such women. What do you say about it?' They said this to test him, and to find a reason for accusing him. But Jesus only bent down and wrote with his finger in the earth. When they continued pressing him with questions, he straightened up and said, 'Whoever among you is free of sin, let him throw the first stone at her.' And again he bent down and wrote in the earth. When they had heard his words, they went out, one by one, beginning with the eldest. In the end, he alone was left, and the woman was still standing in the middle. Then Jesus straightened up and said to her, 'Woman, where are they? Has no one condemned you?' She said, 'No one, Lord.' Then Jesus said, 'I do not condemn you, either. Go, and from now on do not sin any more! (John 8:1–11 JM)

What is happening here? Stoning, which is prescribed by Moses for adultery, is a physical picture or image of the spiritual fact that man collapses under the burden of the objective weight of sin. As with lies so also with adultery there is an objective consequence in the spiritual world that burdens us with guilt. Something has been created by the woman's deed that contributes to a darkening of the world. Executing the Mosaic commandment would have made this fact visible in the stoning of the woman.

Christ transforms the Mosaic law. He forgives: 'I do not condemn you either.' But he can do this only if he takes the guilt upon himself, if he takes the destruction upon himself, if he takes away what otherwise would destroy us.

This is indicated symbolically when Christ bends down to the earth and writes something in it — certainly something connected with the guilt of this woman; for the earth is to become his body. The fact that the woman for her part is not free of all obligations appears at the conclusion with the words, 'Go, and from now on do not sin anymore!'

By taking the *objective* part of sin upon himself, Christ makes it possible for human beings to compensate the *subjective* part themselves. Christ's deed is not insignificant for this realm either. Indeed, Christ does not remove the need for us to compensate, but he encourages and empowers us to 'take up our cross' and to carry it. As we described earlier, healing streams into human beings from Christ. Looking to him, turning to him creates uprightness and encourages the human self to carry its destiny.

From this point of view, the sacrament of confession in its new form in the Christian Community, the Sacrament of Consultation, takes on new meaning. The renewed form of this sacrament can be a genuine help on the path to experiencing more deeply the forgiving power of Christ in one's own life. This sacrament gives one the strength to help him take up his cross and carry it. The strength to learn from any destiny is stimulated. In the light of Christ, man becomes a 'learner' who is increasingly able to take hold of and shape his own life.

Today in the Christian Community, this confession consists of a voluntary conversation with a priest that leads into a sacramental experience of the presence of Christ and prepares one for communion. The blessing takes the form of a strengthening of the human 'I' through Christ.

The blessing that streams from the redemptive power of Christ into single individuals continues and flows through them to others. Christ is never present only for one person, he is present for all people. What an individual receives in his reconciliation with Christ wants to flow further. Turning to Christ in a Christian community should unfold the power to carry not only one's own cross but also the strength to help carry others' crosses. This is one part of what a Christian community is all about. Just as guilt is often not an individual matter but results from mutual aggression, threats, enticements, etc. — that is *common* guilt — so too in the future bearing the consequences of destiny will require the genuine help of other people and establish a deeper experience of community.

One human being's genuine sacrifice for another has profound consequences. What one human being does for another out of devotion and good will — perhaps over years or even decades of faithful caring, or through enduring patiently the other's weaknesses and difficulties — is not done in vain. It can be taken up into destiny as a force that reconciles and dissolves debt, as Paul says, 'Bear one another's burdens' (Gal.6:7). Also in *inner* victories over self — in forgiving, in our struggles with a lack of understanding, antipathy, lovelessness and aggression — forces that dissolve guilt and reconcile can work from one person to another.

What is good?

Perhaps it has become clear that in our time — it may have been different in the past — it is no longer possible to draft a 'catalogue of norms' for good, which applies to every 'good person.' In every life situation good must be sought anew as we saw with the example of how one handles money: at one time, a 'reasonable greed' (thrift), at another time 'extravagance' (a willingness to sacrifice), may be what is appropriate. The golden mean between the two extremes must always be discovered anew.

Neither is good 'normalized' in fairy tales. It only comes into being through courageous or wakeful actions of the hero. Evil is accepted in fairy tales but not lamented, which is not to say that it is assented to. It is seen in the role it plays, for without evil, nothing happens; only danger and trials initiate development. 'The good is developed through evil in fairy tales; it brings about transformation through courageous actions,' as we said earlier. Good, therefore, is not simply given. That is the point that we must stress here once again. In the words of Verena Kast we are dealing with an 'ethic of the path.'

It is increasingly impossible simply to follow a set of external norms. We are called upon to make decisions; that means our 'I' must become active in deciding 'yes' or 'no.' So, too, we must take responsibility for our actions. We have come of age. In the course of our destiny we are learning (our spiritual selves are learning) to take ourselves in hand and freely take up the challenge of destiny.

Of course, in many predicaments of destiny today there is no simple choice between good and evil, often not even any middle path between two forms of one-sidedness. Often we are dealing only with the possibility of doing something that is more or less bad or we must make a compromise. In this regard, individuals can find themselves trapped in situations with no way out, situations in which it is even impossible to recognize anymore what should count as good or evil. It often takes a long time just to figure out exactly what is tangled up in the situation. Nevertheless, in such situations, everything still depends on the attitude with which we stand in them, or the motivations that underlie our next steps. The more strongly I employ my 'good will' and not mere egotism, the sooner I will be able to find the good that lies within the given situation, for this life — or, for a destiny that can only unfold in future lives.

With the term 'ethic of the path' we do not merely mean that evil works as an incentive for evolution and spiritual growth, but also that in hopeless situations good actually only comes into existence through human behaviour. Even in situations where there is nothing to be done but endure hopelessness, good can still be created that never existed before. Of course, this thought does not grant licence for action without scruples. On the contrary, it shows us that much more depends on our attitude during our actions than the way the deed appears to others. Nothing should hold us back from radically striving for good. If we are truly hindered from doing good then it can help to bear in mind that the inner struggle in such situations represents an even higher good.

The 'I' is challenged today to decide for good. It must begin by first creating good in a seemingly difficult, oppressive, hopeless situation. Gradually it will become evident that in the future man will have to become a creative force in the universe. Even though we are only at the beginning of such a development, we can see something of this beginning to become reality in this field of moral decisions.

Of course, we may fail to do good — this possibility is portrayed quite realistically in fairy tales, and it must exist for the sake of human freedom. In keeping with the wisdom of fairy tales we can add, 'Evil brings about transformation through our enduring the suffering that it creates.' Patience and a difficult destiny endured through failures and guilt are clearly seen as powers that transform evil into good. In this way, through human actions, spirit becomes active in the world. Evil brings about transformation. It does so through the force of redemption awakened in our fellow humans. Finally, through Christ, redeeming and reconciling forces can stream into our destiny.

We also find in fairy tales a form of evil so great that it must be avoided. Today especially we are increasingly seeing that there are areas in life where the only appropriate response is to say 'no,' for example, everything having to do with black magic, with drugs or technologies involving radioactivity (at least in warfare).

We have spoken of today's uncertainty with respect to good; but we can also say there are two forces in us that are reliable companions wherever we may stand: selfless love, above all when it is connected to interest in the world, and an honest striving to discover what is right and to do it. Yet even these two forces are no guarantee of a 'good life.' Yet even in the deepest darkness they are able to lead us further.

We have seen a possible path through which evil can be gradually overcome. It cannot be overcome easily or quickly but will require a long evolutionary development. Just as evil has been sinking deeper into mankind for thousands of years, so too the battle to free ourselves from it — which is becoming fully conscious only in our time — will involve long periods of time.

CHAPTER 12

Healing the Sickness of Sin

Various forms of the sickness of sin appear in the biblical account of the Fall as the consequences of disobeying God's commandment. One could easily misunderstand these consequences as punishment for the sins of Adam and Eve. However, it would be disproportionate and senseless to punish humanity so terribly for overstepping a divine command out of ignorance.

The more clearly we understand that the Fall into sin was a spiritual necessity, the more clearly we can view the 'punishing' consequences of sin from a new perspective. They become the consequences of a necessary evolution, which impinge inevitably upon man but as a necessity for the development of humanity.

The word 'punishment' has become loaded with connotations having nothing to do with its beneficial effects. True, these effects are associated with the positive results of pain. If we are not paying attention and walk into a door, the pain associated with the event serves to awaken us and teaches us to be more careful. Actually, that is the point of all pain — to teach and awaken. From this point of view, we can see that the consequences of the Fall into sin are a necessity given by God as a means of education, as medication for the sickness of sin; that is to say, as a means of preventing us from falling completely into the hands of the Adversaries.

This train of thought carried to its conclusion leads us to the following insight: The consequences of the Adversaries' work in human souls actually provide the very means by which the Adversaries can be overcome.

Death: the path to birth of the spirit

Ageing and death are the most horrible consequences of the Ahrimanic influence on the human body. In keeping with this idea, Paul characterized death as the consequence of sin: 'The wages of sin is death' (Rom.6:23). Nevertheless, the double role of the Adversaries shows itself here particularly clearly. Death is the wisdom-filled means by which the spiritual world pulls humans out of their entanglement in earthly existence, allows them to experience the spirit again and gives them another chance in another life on earth.

Seen in this light, death is a benefactor. For what would happen if humans had to dwell eternally in the earthly, trapped in Luciferic and Ahrimanic entanglements, without being able to experience any new impulse from the spirit in their destinies? They would be in danger of falling completely to the Adversaries. But a return to the spiritual world gives them the possibility of a fresh beginning with a different perspective.

However, it is also true that if humans surrender themselves exclusively to materialistic concerns on the earth then they will find it difficult to climb to the higher realms of the spiritual world when they die. A new beginning in their next life on earth is only possible through an experience of those higher realms. As in sleep so also in life after death, they are in danger of not being able to lift themselves to the heights. In the long run, the consequence would be 'the second death,' as it is called in the Apocalypse, the death of the soul — a withering of the innermost part of the human being. Ahriman is counting on it.

So the death of individual humans is the medicine against the cosmic death that threatens the entire earthly realm. We must develop forces in our soul that allow us at death to rise up and cross the threshold into the spiritual. Then death can lead us to a spiritual birth. In the words of Novalis, 'When a spirit dies, he becomes a man. When a man dies, he becomes spirit.'

For Christians, the cross — the symbol of death and resurrection — stands not at the end of life but in the middle. Angelus Silesius said, 'Die before you must die, so that you must not die, when you have to die, otherwise you will face ruin.' Since Christ's passage through death the experience of death for us can also be an inner experience before our external death. Today, such death experiences occur in countless human destinies in the middle of life. They can become key experiences helping us to not 'face ruin.' We are able to push through to a higher life because Christ has overcome death from within, and wants to make the spiritual power of this deed accessible to everyone. Every deed that contains a victory over oneself, that is the overcoming of egotism, shows itself to be a 'die and become' moment in the soul. He who 'takes his cross upon himself' is prepared to live, not only out of his lower, earthly self, but out of his higher self. This requires the sacrifice of one's very own being (as experienced by the lower self) to something higher. Death processes take place in the soul, but they lead to a spiritual birth, to the appearance in the soul of something higher. The instrument of death is taken out of the hand of Ahriman when we voluntarily practise the death of egotism in our souls. Death is torn away from Ahriman through the cross. By freely accepting death, 'in the middle of life' as a deed in the soul realm (what is intended here has nothing to do with suicide) we take away from Ahriman the authority over this process and in this way unite with Christ. Paul points to this with the words, 'I die daily' (1 Cor.15:31), and is speaking of the power to overcome that arises in a person when he practises such dying. Then death itself becomes something different at the end of life: a more conscious entrance into the spiritual world, a conscious experience of the higher life of Christ in death.

Death is preceded by ageing. We are not overlooking the frailty, suffering and pain of a bodily and psychological kind that ageing brings. And yet, what would life be without the overview, the review of things past, the clarification of what was experienced that is possible with age? Something very precious in human life can arise here, a power of wisdom, of love, the ability to bless such as can be found only in old age — especially in the struggle with suffering and frailty.

Ahriman's influence on the physical body in ageing and the descent into death is visibly obvious. However, we have also seen that what appears as a terrible fate for human beings shows itself actually to be a necessary medicine against evil. This is all in keeping with the assertion at the beginning of this chapter that the consequences of the Fall into sin bring with them a kind of therapy for humanity.

The burden of work

The hardening of earthly existence is likewise a consequence of the Fall. We spoke of the terrible burden that has come to human beings: 'In the sweat of your face you shall eat bread.' For countless people today the burden of work is still something of a curse, a punishment. This must not be overlooked or belittled.

Humans only gradually learned to labour on the earth. In distant, ancient times the first humans lived as hunters and gatherers. Shepherding and caring for livestock represents a later stage of development. But humanity only fully put foot on the earth with the cultivation of the soil and thereby began the epoch of true earthly labour.

Work is not only a necessity that makes our earthly existence possible. With every physical action that we carry out in the earthly realm we are also doing something that is not 'external,' something that has real consequences for the earth. Our actions connect us with the earth in a way that has meaning for the future.

The deeper significance of labour is this, that something flows from human actions into earthly substances that makes it possible for the earth to be spiritualized. Material existence is not only shaped externally. Through work human beings also give something inwardly to matter that subtly changes it.

This thought is not entirely remote to human experience. There is something different in the feel of works of art, or even frequently-used everyday objects, if they have been fashioned by human hands rather than produced by machines. Many people today prefer to be surrounded by pieces of furniture that were entirely handmade by craftsmen. We can feel how the love and care of human labour somehow 'imbue' the objects with a spiritual 'substance', which we can then sense.

This experience can be very striking when viewing landscapes that have been 'worked' reverentially by humans for centuries. The atmosphere or aura of such landscapes has been changed. Something similar can be perceived in gardens that have been lovingly cared for. The earth assumes a human gesture. It takes some of the very best of our humanity into itself and is transformed in a human way. What we invest into material existence in this way continues to work through time.

Just as certain earthly substances, such as coal and oil, have stored the energy of the sun from ancient times, substances that can now be transformed into light and warmth, so also in a spiritual sense human soul-forces have been absorbed by earthly matter which has been worked by humans. These forces will be available at a later time as a power to transform everything earthly.

We are reminded of Paul's words: the 'tyranny of transitory existence' (Rom.8:19–23 JM) in creation should be overcome by humans. These words give us an idea of how earthly work should be accomplished.

Mankind will live on a spiritualized earth when the age of the material earth has passed. This earth, which humanity will have won for itself, is where we will continue evolving in the future. This idea is also contained in the New Testament in the picture of the New Jerusalem, the spiritual dwelling of the future in which God and mankind will work together.

What mankind has done to the earth as a result of the Fall into sin, by pulling it down into hardness, becomes at first the 'curse of work,' but this curse can be transformed into a blessing for the earth and for mankind. Knowing this we can be motivated anew to learn how to love the duties presented to us by our daily work.

Spiritualization of the earthly

We can experience the beginning of a spiritualization of material existence in artistic creation. By elevating earthly material to a higher stage, a stage not achievable by natural existence itself, art brings the earthly realm to a place where it can reveal the spiritual.

Art — that is the human ability to lift oneself above what is merely given in the earthly — is a gift from Lucifer. This is a characteristic example of how maintaining the balance between Ahrimanic and Luciferic extremes gives us an opportunity for development. When Lucifer gave us the ability to use our artistic capacities in order to rise above the Ahrimanic fetters to the earthly, which Paul called 'the tyranny of transitory existence,' he also gave us the ability freely to shape and form earthly substance. Such artistic creation can cause the spiritual to appear in the earthly. When this happens, there is an encounter from two directions: the earthly is lifted up above its natural level and the spiritual is made visible so that it becomes perceptible and can be experienced by earthly humans. One transforms the Ahrimanic, the other the Luciferic one-sidedness. It is human being who brings about this transformation.

In the realm of art we see an influx of spiritual forces of the most varied kind into earthly existence. This leads us to the question of whether humans could perhaps bring an artistic element to *everything* they touch. Manual human labour could be shaped more consciously so that work would not be such a burden in the future, but could itself become more 'human,' even in technical processes. If the renewal that anthroposophy seeks in the cultural realm can unfold further, then this idea could become a reality. There are the beginnings of this in many areas. Something will flow into human labour that goes beyond the fact-orientated, earthly-given and can make the specifically human capacities of human beings effective in the world. If the artistic process could permeate the entire world of labour then the one-sidedness of labour would be ameliorated. Furthermore, the creative power to shape, form and spiritualize that comes from humans could be carried into the areas of technology and administration, areas that are in large measure closed to them today.

The Christian ritual of the Eucharist speaks of the highest spiritualization of the earthly. When bread and wind are transformed, that is spiritualized in the Christian Eucharist they represent more than a picture or a symbol. If natural existence is to be led back to a higher level of being in the sense Paul spoke of, then this development must take place somewhere. This happens when the ritual or cultus is celebrated. Bread and wine are lifted out of the 'tyranny of earthly existence' in an archetypal fashion — receptive, transparent for the presence of Christ. They can be elevated to his 'body,' in that the power of Christ 'sinks' into them and makes them into a place for his presence that works into his earthly-bodily substance of bread and wine.

The word 'cultus' comes from the Latin *colere* which means 'to cultivate the land' and 'to work' in the highest sense. We can also understand cultus as art in the highest sense. What is at work in a symphony is an arrangement of 'earthly materials,' of tones, rhythms, volume, etc., that reveal a quality pointing beyond the earthly. For example, when music by Mozart, Beethoven, Bruckner or Bach, sounds forth, especially when performed with great devotion, a door opens to a higher spiritual realm.

Similarly, the Christian ritual contains 'earthly material' and reveals a certain arrangement of words, gestures, colours, and substances etc. which, when permeated by specific rhythms and intense devotion, can become the bearer of a spiritual revelation. Just as a chord within a symphony can reveal a special power to illuminate the composition because it appears at just the right place in the context of the musical event, so also in cultus bread and wine reveal a special power hidden in everyday existence, which enables them to become a revelation of the body and blood of Christ.

Celebrating the Christian cultus with its transformation of bread and wine into the body and blood of the divine son can become the highest, divine 'art,' in which God wants to be revealed. Cultus can be experienced as a model and archetype for the earthly task of every human being, which is *to carry spirit into the earthly*, even into our daily work. In this way it can be an encouragement and a source of strength.

We can also see in it a first sign of the redemption of the earthly from the Fall into matter. Earthly substance can be raised up from its Fall and carried over into a higher realm of being. Hence, part of Ahriman's intervention can be healed in the Christian ritual.

Every properly-celebrated Christian ritual represents a healing. When bread and wine are received by the congregation in the Lord's Supper, in Communion, we can think of this as the beginning of a healing that reaches all the way into our earthly, bodily nature.

In art and in ritual we can experience how the spirit reaches into the earthly in a transforming way and how we can receive the power of transformation for our own earthly deeds. This transforming power is hidden in human work and will show itself later as a seed for transforming the earth.

Technology: not a means of healing, but a means of help

Broadly speaking, labour today is not thinkable without technology. It represents an entirely different world from art. Here too the earthly is not left in its original form; technology can bring about transformation, which we should perhaps call 'change.' Here too spirit imprints the earthly. But what kind of a spirit?

Everything connected with technology can appear to represent the opposite of the artistic process. It negates, disrespects and supplants the very humanity of human beings. Yet ever since the first stone tool was fashioned, technology has developed through many stages and brought us, above all, the possibility of liberation from the burden of work.

So much has been written about the shadow side of technical development that we can forego a discussion here. It is easy to recognize the Ahrimanic one-sidedness in technology. All technology is based on the laws of the physical world including the application of electricity, magnetism and nuclear physics, increasingly without regard for the realm of the living or the realm of the soul. We recognize the kingdom of Ahriman. Technology can develop enormous forces from this region of the physical-earthly and put them to work serving humanity. We see in this some of the awesome might of Ahrimanic powers. Technology is based on the development of extraordinary intelligence, to the point of computers acquiring an apparent independence. We can get a feeling for the awesome magnitude of the *super-intelligence* possessed by Ahrimanic powers, which are entirely soulless. The development and significance of today's machines have absolutely nothing to do with any specific abilities of the soul. Driving a car, using a washing machine, or a carpenter's bench can take place independently of all that I am as a human being. The situation is different for the work of a teacher, nurse or farmer, etc. where we recognize that Ahrimanic powers stand *outside all human feeling and experience.*

Such statements are not in principle directed against the use of technology. There is also a need for the development of technology. However, this necessity is at the same time a challenge for us to develop higher forces and insights. The rapid development of technology cannot and should not be rejected. However, it is clear to many people today that we need to set limits to technology so that everything human is not pushed aside, and so technology can serve us.

Technology also shows us a side that we can experience as an intensification of the 'curse of work' brought about by Ahrimanic forces. Despite its burden, human labour done by hand nevertheless has something satisfying for the worker. This positive aspect is gone in the technical world of work. Man serves the machine, which imposes its own work rhythm on him; it suppresses all initiative, alienates us from ourselves and the world. Not only does this kind of work take our energy from us, but increasingly such work is simply not enough for us to feel that our lives are complete.

In the future, decisive changes will have to be made so that we can again experience some satisfaction in the work we do. On the other hand, we are challenged by this intensification of Ahrimanic one-sidedness not merely to surrender ourselves as victims to technical development, but we must set reasonable aims for it and above all we must compensate for it with a further evolution of our human and moral abilities. Those whose work requires them to be involved with technical processes or who drive a lot are thereby called upon to cultivate spiritual development and artistic activities. The extreme one-sidedness of our civilization should become a painful incentive to progress on our way to full humanity.

However, today there is also an increasing possibility for us to be liberated from the slavery of external work, to be free for meaningful activities. Leisure time is being created to an extent never seen before. Leisure time also brings a challenge to use the additional time properly, not just for consuming but for creative activity. We are just barely able to do this today; in the future it will certainly be a major social problem. This challenge must also lead to the individual engaging himself much more intensely as a spiritual and creative being.

The continued development of technology has led to another threat to our humanity — unemployment. It has suddenly made it clear how important work is for humans, how terrible a destiny is to be condemned to 'doing nothing.' It will require a great deal of insight and imagination in the social realm to assure every man and woman the necessary quantum of work, and it will be recognized just what a blessing it is to have work that is appropriate for one's individual development. Through work we 'get moving' in life. In the encounter with the environment on all levels — in thinking, for work must be done properly, meaningfully; in will, for work means action and initiative — the 'I' of the human being is set in motion. It encounters the world and itself. Above all, through external work the 'I' — at least in a preliminary way — is stripped of the subjectivity that Lucifer set it in. For work leads into the realm of objective facts.

To summarize: with the Fall into sin, humanity was condemned to work on the earth. This means not only a curse and punishment but above all a remedy for the temptations of Lucifer. Again we see 'evil' in its dual roles. The question as to whether the ill-fated appearance of the sickness of sin might also contain a positive side for humanity can, for two important areas, be answered in the affirmative.

The meaning of illness

Illness, pain and frailty are Ahrimanic effects of the Fall in the sphere of the life body. Is there perhaps something also here that we can recognize as 'medication?' It can be quite surprising, even moving, to witness how, in human destiny, illness and infirmity work to help an individual to mature as a human being.

It also requires deep knowledge of how destinies can unfold to understand a destiny that must bear severe or lifelong illness, not to mention cases of severe disability.

We can recognize many illnesses as the self-incurred consequence of someone's earlier behaviour. Cirrhoses of the liver in an alcoholic, for example, is clearly a result of the person's actions — in this case the misuse of alcohol — in this earth life. Let us consider this example: is the liver illness a 'punishment' for human misbehaviour, for a 'sin?' Or could this signify something else?

We can only proceed in the way previously indicated. Illness is a means of education employed by our destiny to strengthen and consolidate us in those areas of our soul in which we are weak. Therefore every illness has a specific meaning for the one afflicted.

Sometimes this process of strengthening and consolidation becomes visible in the maturation described earlier. For example, cirrhoses of the liver in an alcoholic may be associated with a great deal of suffering, but it may not always be perceptible that the severely ill person is maturing because of it. Is it all for nothing, then? Not at all, for in enduring and suffering the disease, forces arise that are taken into the life after death where they develop further, and can then be carried over into a new life. So that then something of the weakness that led to alcoholism can be overcome, or at least a strong will develops in the soul to overcome it.

A weakness of the soul and the 'I' led to a fall into alcoholism — this weakness is a result of Lucifer's work in mankind. It then draws the disease (the work of Ahriman) after it. But this is then used by good powers if destiny to heal and strengthen the soul against future Luciferic and Ahrimanic attacks.

For the diseases and infirmity that do not obviously have any misbehaviour as a cause in this life, the question naturally arises whether the cause might lie in a past earth life. If we think at all of former incarnations then we must also include the possibility of all different kinds of errors, injustice, misdeeds, as deeds and sins of omission. They came forth in the past from the soul's weakness or error that was not allowed to continue if the person was not to fall any deeper into the hands of the Adversaries. So disease becomes the destiny for the next earth life, disease that is able to compensate for the soul's weakness. Again, this is not 'punishment' for past sins but rather an aid to strengthen the inner human being.

The truth of disease and infirmity as consequences and remedy for past weakness can be quite unsettling, even disturbing. We must remember that before birth we were in agreement, out of a higher wisdom, with our forthcoming destiny, indeed we ourselves helped to choose it. This truth is one of the most important in the field destiny: our destiny comes to us through our own decision and not from outside.

Furthermore, let us remember that not all destiny must be determined from the past. Some is determined by what is yet to come from the future. A heavy destiny and much suffering sometimes comes to us so that we may develop strength for the future. This may well be true for many destinies involving illness today.

Greater social concern

We have described the human attachment to the digestive system and the need for nourishment — the second impairment of the etheric body — as a dual effect of Lucifer and Ahriman, which human beings cannot escape. Are there any positive aspects to this enslavement?

The need to eat implies the need to work, for without the need to satisfy our hunger and quench our thirst, an essential incentive to work would be missing. As we have seen, work is necessary to strengthen and objectify the 'I.' Indirectly this represents a positive effect of mankind's need for nourishment.

There are perspectives for the future, too. Will social interactions improve in the future? Will a new understanding of nourishment, with a resulting new approach to handling all forms of foodstuffs, arise in the future?

An enhanced experience of community should also include our relationship to the earth and the animal kingdom. Until now the principle of radical exploitation has held sway.

The earth is already beginning to respond with decreased fertility. We are increasingly threatened by water shortages, pollution, diminished crop yields, etc. A fundamental rethinking is unavoidable and has already shown signs of having begun.

We are seeing a further Ahrimanic attack on nature, through human actions. We ourselves are spoiling the earth today. Our blindness causes us to aid Ahrimanic powers.

External measures alone — reducing air pollution, for example — will no longer achieve very much. What will be decisive is an increased consciousness of our social connection with everything, including the earth. We need awareness accompanied by corresponding actions that the earth is not a dead something that can be exploited, but rather an ensouled being who is ready to carry and nourish humanity but not prepared to participate in all our egotism.

Biodynamic agriculture has taken up the indications given by Rudolf Steiner in this field. Although the beginnings are quite modest, seeds capable of further development have been planted: responsibility for the earth, for enlivening it and for its greater fruitfulness.

New opportunities, insights and paths in this field have come from a knowledge of the earth's essential life. We can hope that the development of these insights can guarantee humanity a life on the earth in the future. The increase in the earth's population is due to the fact that human souls need to experience just this time in history because it is so important. However, we cannot expect the 'population explosion' to continue. The new beginnings in treating the earth and her soil with wisdom and respect represent a first medication to heal Ahriman's power of death.

However, this alone is not sufficient without an increased sense of community among humans. Rudolf Steiner said that in the future, humans will not be able to experience their own happiness independently from the happiness of other people. Besides the crass egotism we meet today, we also encounter the beginnings of social sensitivity in the coming generation. Perhaps a great social consciousness will grow out of this sensitivity so that we develop not only an 'environmental awareness' but an 'awareness of the people in our environment.' We would then instinctively feel not only our own needs, but the needs of other people. This would bring the aforementioned medication against Ahriman (and Lucifer) to full effectiveness. We hardly have any alternative — at most, the 'war of all against all.' That, however, is no alternative but rather an intensified threat to all that is human. This threat must become an incentive for us to evolve further. Thus, hunger and thirst can fulfill a mission above and beyond themselves, a mission that leads humanity forward.

Between animal and angel

To a certain extent, man's form of nourishment is an advanced, 'refined' version of the way animals eat. This point of view, which is justified to some extent, must, however, be supplemented by a spiritual worldview. We can think of a scene in the Gospels reported in John 4.

The disciples have left Christ at a well in the fields and have gone into the city to buy bread. When they return and want to give him something to eat he says: 'I have food to eat of which you do not know ... My food is to do the will of him who sent me, and to accomplish his work' (John 4:31–34).

In the realm of angels and archangels there is also an exchange of substance, a participation in the divine love, by which spiritual beings are built up and from which they live. In a similar way, we must imagine the creation, building up and enlivening of man in paradise.

In his paradisal state, man participated in the 'nourishment of the gods.' When he distanced himself from divine love and fell out of the divine will, he fell down into the condition in which he still finds himself. Yet even today, the process of human digestion is not entirely bound to the material. Today we are learning to judge food not only according to its calorific content but also in terms of its biological value — that is according to its life-forces and the health they can promote. Just because an apple looks healthy does not mean that it is, especially if it has been treated with deleterious chemicals. We are beginning to pay attention to the forces that actually nourish in foods. Their presence depends upon whether the life-forces in plants have been weakened or made unusable for our bodies by chemicals. Then they do not truly nourish but actually weaken us. Many illnesses and weakened constitutions today are caused or partly caused by food whose life-forces have been reduced in this way.

Yet even in this field where people have learned to demand healthier food, egotism often immediately comes into play. We can oppose this egotism by saying a prayer before meals. The efficacy of grace before meals is related to Christ's words, 'Man does not live by bread alone but by every word that comes from the mouth of God' (Matt.4:4 RSV).

It is definitely not easy for us today to see grace before meals as a reality. To do so we need to remember experiences from times of war and hunger. In such situations many have experienced what it means to eat bread with gratitude and devotion. One can feel another dimension of nourishment; small amounts of food become merely a 'door' through which nourishing spiritual forces can enter one's body.

Grace before meals, looking up to the worlds that truly maintain and enliven us, is a powerful, even if entirely unconscious, reality. A spiritual process weaves into earthly digestion. In the future, mankind will become more conscious of the fact that with the proper inner attitude, earthly nourishment can recede while our life-forces in the physical body are nevertheless maintained. The external process of digestion will then only become the occasion, the stimulation, the entryway for other spiritual processes. 'Man will not live from bread alone.'

All of this may lie far in the future, and yet this future is being prepared in our time. A different relationship to nourishment must begin, not just in terms of healthy eating — which easily becomes egotistical — but in the sense indicated above. Grace at meals is a genuine beginning for this process of uniting thankfulness and devotion with our daily mealtimes. It gives us a chance to feel, at least for a moment, the holiness of the event.

In this way, we are raised above the animal and remind ourselves that human nourishment can be an image of the 'nourishment of the gods,' that in every meal there is something of this higher nourishment. A real culture of table manners, of a table set for celebration, and carefully-prepared meals lift the process up to the angels.

With the way we eat and drink we can sink to the level of animals — then we are following the guidance of Ahrimanic powers. However, we can also raise ourselves above the level of the human. Then spiritual forces flow into our daily life.

The Christian Eucharist, the mass, raises eating and drinking to the level of angels. Receiving bread and wine becomes 'the revelation of God's love' to human beings. And human devotion to the will of God is manifested in the sense of Christ's words, 'My food is to do the will of him who sent me.'

The amount of food in the Eucharist is very little but it is woven into a mighty ritual. Hence, we can behold the picture described above of a future form of human nourishment. At the same time we have here the counterpart to the image of Adam and Eve eating the forbidden fruit in paradise, the event that led to the entire Fall into sin. The Lord's Supper brings spiritual forces that work to compensate for and heal the sickness of sin.

Conceiving and knowledge

We must also include perspectives that reach far into the future when we deal with questions concerning human sexuality. There is a discrepancy between human desire and its fulfilment; sexuality itself can only be a stimulus for fulfilment but cannot itself constitute the deeper fulfilment sought by the human soul. The power of human sexuality actually has a deeper task that is only fulfilled in the act of knowing.

Stephan Leber has worked out the fundamental connection between these two human activities.[1] The Bible itself characterizes what is meant here with the Hebrew word for 'knowing' when it is used for the act of conceiving: 'Adam knew his wife and she bore' (Gen.4:1). There are twelve other occurrences in the Old Testament with corresponding usage.

We also find the same usage in the New Testament when it is said of Joseph that, 'he knew her not' (Matt.1:25) and when Mary says, 'I know not a man' (Luke 1:34). In each instance a Greek word is used which otherwise clearly means the act of knowing, for example in the first chapter of Luke a few verses before the words of Mary just quoted, when Zacharias asks, 'How shall I *know* this?' — that is the truth of the angel's message (Luke 1:18). Each time the Greek word is ginosko, which means 'to know.'

At that time in history, people still had some awareness of the fact that deeper forces of knowledge are truly connected with the forces active in reproduction. Rudolf Steiner actually said,

> All the organs of growth and reproduction are metamorphosed
> sense organs that have been taken hold of by the etheric body.[2]

In response to Steiner's words, Stefan Leber says:

> What should these organs perceive? Not images of some reality,
> but the real essence of something hidden directly behind the
> appearances ... accordingly the Gospel uses the term 'to know'
> for sexual union ... This also points out that, in addition to
> the actual reproductive function, the sexual organs still retain
> something of their original function: the perception of another
> person at the deepest level of being.

Even though the 'act of knowledge' stated here will usually remain deeply unconscious, nevertheless the idea developed points in the only direction in which human sexuality can find fulfilment: love that points beyond sexuality to another human being, a love that seeks to lead to deeper knowledge.

Destiny or karmic relationships

Beyond all the problems associated with the realm of sexuality there are three motifs that can show us the work of the positive spiritual forces:

1. Destiny relationships arise;
2. It is possible for children to be born so that additional souls can have a destiny on earth;
3. In marriages that are cultivated and properly carried forces for the future can arise.

Let us consider the first point. The tension between the sexes becomes a means of uniting two people who belong together. The powers that guide human destiny make use of these powerful tensions to bind people together who have a deep common destiny. It is easy to see something beginning to work that leads beyond one's own egotism. It is an impulse to be interested not only in oneself but also in other people, to unite with them — in marriage, friendship, common interest, to learn from them, suffer, often to walk a difficult path with them. Without the impulse meant here, which can express itself in all the various ways sympathy (and antipathy) can play out, many of the factors that connect people in destiny would be very weak or missing entirely.

Here we come to the knowledge aspect of sexual forces from another side. For me to recognize in an encounter of destiny — and I do not mean here those of a superficial kind — that a person belongs in my destiny and to recognize this more or less clearly: a common destiny is at work here — this is an act of knowledge. The expression 'love is blind' must be supplemented by the observation that it might make us blind for someone's weaknesses, but it also makes it possible for us to see the virtues and the uniqueness of another person. Without love it is not possible to truly know anyone.

So we see the power of sexuality, despite the difficulties associated with it, in the service of human development. This is even clearer when we consider it as an entrance for souls seeking a new destiny on the earth, that is when children come. It casts yet another light on the unfathomable depths of these powers: they have the power to attract human souls (this is not meant in the sense of compulsion) and to prepare for them an appropriate body. The sexual act of leading to conception is like a signal to the soul striving towards incarnation that access to earth is possible with his or her predestined parents. The soul takes hold of this opportunity and pregnancy results.

Again we are dealing with the process of knowing. In this case it is the soul descending out of the spiritual world into incarnation whose 'knowing' is the perception of an opportunity to unite with an earthly body. It also recognizes the parents belonging to that incarnating soul and who will make an earthly destiny possible. The preview of our life destiny, that takes place long before birth, includes finding the best possible parents necessary for our unique needs — the proper environment and genetic inheritance. The soul seeks its parents. A child that announces its coming through pregnancy wants to come to these parents.

As we have said, there is knowledge of a deeper sort in these events. The reverse perspective (from parents) also includes a kind of knowledge. There is a deeply unconscious 'divining' present in the more or usually less conscious 'will towards a child' that leads to conception. This divining is a dim awareness that a soul is on its way, that a child wants to come.

Furthermore, all that the mother, and sometimes the father, can experience in terms of intuitions, moods, occasionally clear images or insights (e.g. certain knowledge of the name) belong to the realm of deeper powers of knowledge in the sense here intended.

We see the whole wonderful complex of connections involved with the question of children. We are dealing with the realm of life-forces in the widest sense — forces that have been attached and made unfree in two ways by the Adversaries — which, nevertheless, serve the cause of human evolution and growth.

In spiritual science, life-forces are also called 'formative forces.' They have the power to shape and form a human body; but they also form the threads of destiny and the complex 'net of destiny' that make it possible for us to evolve. These forces reach into the heights of pre-birth existence and — in their effects — into our life after death.

Marriage

The third motif, marriage, is put into question in many regards today. We need not expand on this fact here but will briefly discuss one fundamental point of view.

We have seen that through the Fall into sin, that the original unity of the human being was torn apart. The masculine-feminine being, which, according to the biblical account before the Fall, was already a polarity, though not yet in a disharmonious relationship, was split completely apart into a duality. Ever since then harmony between the sexes must constantly be sought anew. The one-sidedness thereby created applies not only to the physical body, but also to the life body. The life body is formed differently in men and women. The separation of the sexes works to create opposites also in the realm of the life-forces. Will that always remain so?

From the point of view of spiritual science this question is not only justified but also has an answer. In this regard, marriage can be seen as contributing to the further development of humanity. For the bodily union of two people is not only a physical process, but above all is an intimate interpenetration of the life-forces of a man and a woman. The life bodies of a man and a woman experience an intensive exchange of etheric forces. This creates something they have in common, a 'community of life,' which is a reality.

The ring, the symbol of marriage, expresses this, representing a harmonious, perfect union of opposites. Above and below, right and left, are combined in an enclosed unity. The ring was broken, so to speak, in the Fall into sin. It can be re-established in marriage in a preliminary way — at least as far as concerns the life-forces. The oppositional life-forces of man and woman, in living together, create a third, common entity that includes the separated forces.

If the separation of the sexes is to be overcome in the future in an enduring way, then there must be preparation. The formative forces in the life bodies of men and women not only create a foundation for the growth of a new human body, not only the possibility for shaping and forming common human destiny, they also have another task. Every marriage that is rightly carried produces a 'model' for the human being of the future in whom the opposites will again be unified. With the word 'model' we mean an active potency — a configuration of formative forces that will be active in the future.

This potency is created — at least in its initial form — in every situation where a man and a woman live together — not merely in a legal marriage. It is possible to feel its presence because every community of life created by two people that is carried by love creates a field of creative possibilities. A sphere of life is formed, which can lend 'living space' and stimulation not only to the couple's own children, but also to many other people.

We realize how much struggle and crisis accompany such living spaces today. The tragedy unfolding in this field is often unimaginable. Nevertheless, there are marriages — and may their number increase in the future — in which what has been described here is a reality.

Marriage is the appropriate place for the forces here described to unfold; for they need quiet cultivation and maturation. They can also begin to develop in other forms of community life, but only when a community of life endures and is carried by the partners' will to work through problems and use them to deepen their togetherness. Only when it matures in this way can the 'ring of life' ripen into the gold of eternity. If the togetherness breaks apart then the ring that had begun to form also breaks.

Hopefully, it has become clear that human powers of reproduction are among the highest gifts entrusted to humanity:
— for the creation of new bodies for human beings to live on earth;
— for creating fields of destiny based on deep knowledge of destiny;
— for the very future of humanity.

The highest possibility is also the highest responsibility and therefore this realm is hotly contested by the Adversaries. However, in the middle of all these problems arising from the Fall into sin, there are positive creative forces for which marriage appears to be the proper 'living space.'

Marriage can form a protected space that life-forces need for their healthy development just as all life needs protection and fostering. And if we are dealing here with forces that are as far-reaching and significant as we have described, it may appear understandable that the spiritual world has great interest in the proper handling of these forces. We can regard marriage in a 'community of life' between two people, as their private affair. However, no one would deny that the joys and woes of a marriage also have unsuspected consequences for other people, even for communities; that a marriage has social consequences in many directions. The development of children is fostered or hindered, usually decisively influenced by the good or bad relationship between the marriage partners. Furthermore, this relationship plays into their professional life and every other community they may be a part of. From this point of view, we can no longer call marriage a private affair. It concerns society in a very significant way and every human community that rightly understands the laws of its own development will want to grant every possible protection to marriage.

In light of this, the Christian Sacrament of Marriage can be understood anew. In this sacrament the spiritual world, as well as the community of people around the couple, is interested in the marriage's success. All three regions in which living formative forces are at work in a community of life — incarnation of human souls, formation of destiny, possibilities for the future:
— are connected with the work of the spiritual beings on earth.
— are the beings who send human souls to earth;
— are at work in human destinies on earth;
— take up the future directed forces that arise in humanity for future development.

In the Sacrament of Marriage we find a manifestation of the spiritual world that seeks to unite its forces with the 'togetherness' of two people, with their marriage; furthermore, the couple themselves reveal that they seek to 'perceive' this manifestation.

All Christian sacramental acts develop something directed against the effects of the Adversaries in human physical and life bodies. Sacramental acts work to heal the sickness of sin. This is very clear in the Last Anointing which reaches into the sphere of death. We have already discussed how Communion with bread and wine raises our earthly nourishment to a higher stage, completes it and leads it further. Baptism and Confirmation also strive to give the human being forces, which save him from sinking too deeply into the earthly. The Ordination of Priests will be discussed in the next section and the significance of the Sacrament of Consultation for anyone struggling with the effects of the Adversaries' work has already been mentioned.

What has already been said concerning cultus in general applies also to the Sacrament of Marriage: it carries Christ's blessing into earthly life. Something is created and appears in earthly pictures and words, something which points beyond the earthly, which originates in the deed of Christ — so it is expressed at the beginning of the wedding sacrament. What arises in this way as a living seed in the sacrament seeks to unite with the destiny of the two. It needs to be developed and cultivated. If the couple can take into their 'readiness to sacrifice' what stems from Christ's sacrifice, it will bring about good and be connected in the right way with the life-forces of the individuals involved.

Of course, the wedding sacrament cannot be seen as a guarantee for the success of a marriage. Today nothing in the spiritual realm will work without the conscious participation of humans. The presence of spiritual beings can however be experienced like the helping presence of a best friend, whose comfort, advice, interest and guidance are always available if we open ourselves to it. However, this friend in his closeness does not want to be forgotten.

Prayer and cultus or ritual are the means by which we can convince ourselves repeatedly of the closeness of our friend. Cultus means 'constructive cultivation,' precisely the cultivation of those forces that are connected with the human life body. The living space of a marriage needs such care and the life found in ritual can grant it.

Job today

The sense world is the only reality we perceive today, for this we can thank the Ahrimanic influence. We have become blind and deaf to the presence of the spiritual world which surrounds us with just as much reality as the physical world; actually it is even more real. For the physical world is a derived reality, derived from the spiritual world.

This truth contradicts completely our present-day experience of reality. We experience the earthly world as the most real. Everything that is spiritual is for us a questionable reality which we can doubt and deny — one of Ahriman's fundamental effects. Our eyes are opened to the physical and closed for the spiritual.

This too must be seen as a result of the Fall into sin. So the question arises here, can something positive be associated with this fact?

We need to bear in mind that human beings would never have found themselves if they had remained connected to the spiritual world through ancient clairvoyance. Self-discovery out of one's own forces had to (and must continue to) occur. For this purpose, ancient vision into the spiritual had to be eclipsed. But our present state of affairs will not last forever either. One could say that in our present time the darkness is beginning to lift. New insights into the spiritual world are increasing. Humanity has matured to the point where it can find its way out of the darkness and into the light.

This is the result of humanity's suffering, which has led to a great longing for its origin in the spirit. We are reminded here of Job who finally came to understand that his suffering must have a higher meaning, that God would not otherwise be so concerned with him, and that there was someone in the spiritual world who could help him. We have seen how his suffering even gave him the strength to break through to a vision of God. 'I had heard of you only with my ears, but now my eyes have seen you!' So also our suffering should not be in vain. We are to gradually arrive at a new vision of Christ and at an understanding of our own deepest being. We are experiencing the beginning of that now. Already today the presence of Christ is, for moments, sometimes perceptible for individual humans. 'The second coming' of Christ, which is nothing more than the experience of his presence is taking place today.

Such experiences will increase. The door to the spiritual world will slowly open again. Just as the Fall into sin long ago transformed the whole human being into something earthly, so we can hope for a future that will bring us again closer to the spirit and transform us in the direction of the spirit.

In the past there was a danger that the human 'I' could be extinguished by the overpowering presence of God. Today it no longer exists. Just as steel can be hardened to withstand extraordinary stress, so too the sufferings of humanity have 'hardened' the 'I' in us and given it the strength to endure the presence of the divine if only for brief moments. We can 'stand before the Son of Man' (Luke 21:36).

The Sacrament of the Ordination of Priests has been established to lead humanity out of the spiritual blindness in which it finds itself, and to awaken an experience of the spiritual world. Within the renewed rituals of the Christian Community, Ordination is directly connected to the Second Coming of Christ and to the awakening of a new vision.

To summarize, we have discussed the forms in which the sickness of sin appears, and have seen the positive aspects hidden within them.

— In ageing and death we have the possibility of maturity and rebirth.

— In the hardening of the earth, which necessitates physical work, we have the possibility to transform the earth and mankind; technology gives us an incentive to find and develop our true humanity.

— In sickness, pain, and infirmity we have the possibility of acquiring inner strength and energy for future tasks.

— In hunger and thirst we have an incentive to create greater social consciousness with respect to the earth and human communities. These needs can also lead us to discover a different, more natural and responsible way to deal with the nourishing forces that come from the earth.

— In human sexuality, out of all the complex problems that plague humanity in this area, we can experience the highest forces that unite us with the spiritual world.

— In the blindness for everything spiritual we can find an incentive to achieve a new vision.

The consequences of the Fall into sin are, therefore, not simply a 'punishment.' When consciously taken hold of and transformed they actually contain the very means by which we can overcome the sickness of sin.

CHAPTER 13

The Human Being in the Future

In the course of our discussion we have repeatedly encountered the idea of man's future. How far does this future extend? We speak of an individual human being having a 'normal' life span and yet we also know that a shortened life span is possible. Today mankind is in danger of having a shortened lifespan even though important epochs, additional millennia of development, are planned for us by the spiritual powers guiding our evolution. Anthroposophy speaks in detail concerning this further evolution.

The crises afflicting humanity today correspond with the crises of maturity facing people in their forties. Important additional years of development await an individual after these middle years of life. There is still much to be experienced unless special circumstances shorten one's life. So too, humanity still has profound stages of development before it. Millennia of humanity's childhood and youth lie behind us. We can speak of humanity having 'grown-up' since approximately the time of Christ. Yet the actual maturation for our life as *human* beings is beginning only now. It should lead us to a further future through thousands of years.

Our present cultural epoch, which began with the Renaissance in the fifteenth century will extend until approximately the middle of the fourth millennium.[1] It will then be followed by the next two-thousand-year epoch that will lead into the sixth millennium. Then another two-thousand-year epoch will conclude an even larger cycle of cultural development (approximately fifteen thousand years). This final epoch will then produce great changes in all earthly circumstances and bring strong impulses for the spiritualization of humanity.

However, earth's evolution will not yet be at an end. The development of the earth and humanity will continue in two additional cycles of development. These ages will be necessary in order to fully transform and spiritualize the earthly and to permit human souls to participate in the right way in these transformations.

This transformation will bring about the penetration of the earthly into the spiritual forces, described in detail in the last chapter. Only at the end of these two great cycles of time will the end of the earth's entire development be reached. Humanity's future beyond the conclusion of earth's evolution stands before us in the apocalyptic picture of the 'New Jerusalem.'

Until then the individual human being and mankind altogether will be able to take further continuous steps towards the goal. There are, therefore, great spans of time available to humanity to achieve its goals.

Speaking of such far-reaching goals can only be meaningful in light of vast expanses of time in which to achieve them. On the other hand, this vast expanse of time has already begun! The essential impulse for the spiritualization of humanity takes place not thousands of years in the future, but right now in our time. Indeed, it has begun with the aforementioned awakening to a new experience of God and a new experience of the spiritual world. From this experience we receive a strong impulse to turn to the spiritual world and to Christ, and to unite ourselves again with the forces of the spirit. This will open entirely new, higher possibilities of insight and give us new powers of will. But we must not forget that further crises and trials still await us. Not only will the advancing part of humanity become stronger, more capable and mature, but the Adversaries' attempts to draw individuals and groups to them will necessarily also increase. However, it can also be said, in the words of Rudolf Steiner:

> The most powerful, flaming words of inspiration spoken today
> will be small and weak compared to what will be at work in
> the future ... we are standing at the beginning of a spiritual
> movement and it will grow; it will require much stubbornness
> and hardness of heart to keep one's heart and soul closed to the
> mighty impressions that will come in the future ... the spiritual
> movement will be formed into a mighty spiritual fire in the
> future.[2]

All these perspectives on the future depend, of course, on the further evolution of humanity itself. If we were now to be at the end of our possibilities, then even the longest span of time would not signify any real future. We would remain as we are.

However, in various ways we have described how much God has 'invested' in man, which will be developed in the future. We find ourselves therefore agreeing with the creation account in the Bible — in light of man's creation in the 'image and likeness of God,' which is still entirely hidden — and also in agreement with many statements in the New Testament. 'It does not yet appear, what we shall be' (1John 3:2).

The hope that we have a great future ahead of us is justified. It begins in our time — as we have already emphasized — with the first unfolding of new spiritual abilities and experiences. The development of such future forces has to do with the evolution of additional 'members' of the human constitution. These are 'aspects' or 'parts' of the human being that are undeveloped and still hidden today. The development of these higher forces is at the same time what we have described as the 'creation of the new Adam.'

Suppression, sublimation and transformation

When we turn to the spiritual world we are allowing higher forces to work into our 'natural' human being. These forces weave something into us that is active in changing and transforming the members of our being. This can be illustrated schematically:

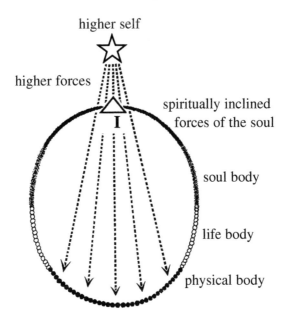

In this schematic (p. 159) we can see that from the realm of the higher self, with the help of the soul-forces that are inclined to the spirit (devotion, reverence, thankfulness, faith, willingness to sacrifice, etc.) and the ability to learn and to practise these forces, something higher can shine into the soul, life and body. However, this higher something would not be higher if it remained inactive and ineffective. So every turning to the spirit is effective in us, even if very quietly. We can show in a further illustration below how the spiritual forces shining into the human being also transform and create:

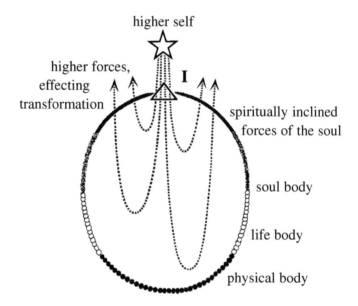

higher self

higher forces, effecting transformation

I

spiritually inclined forces of the soul

soul body

life body

physical body

The transformation of the forces belonging to the lower members of the human constitution raise these forces up above themselves and then form a sheath for the higher human being. The work of the 'I' calls forth their slow transformation. Through the work of the 'I' on the soul-forces (astral body) they are transformed into a higher soul body (also called 'spirit self' by Rudolf Steiner) in which the forces of evil can have no part. Likewise the life-forces (etheric body) are transformed into a 'higher' life and the physical body is transformed into a spiritualized body (Resurrection body). A schematic presentation of this is given opposite.

This last diagram expresses how something of the higher human being is slowly created out of the transformation of the lower members of the human constitution. The 'I' gets mastery of the house by

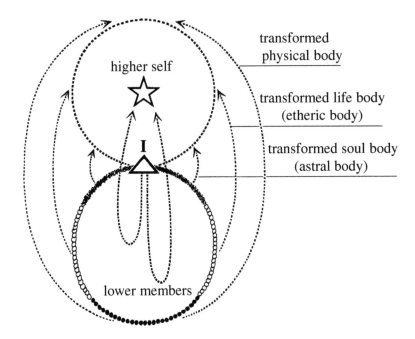

simultaneously creating the appropriate sheaths itself. Indeed, the transformation is beginning above all with the soul-forces. Every conscious choice we make today (i.e. which our 'I' makes) for the good, the beautiful and the true in our thinking, feeling and will gradually transforms our souls.

Man could not come forth from the hand of God in finished form. Man was only possible as a 'draft' of a story only he himself can write to completion and into reality. Until now only the first beginnings have appeared. We are required to create ourselves further, with the help of Christ and of other people. But the decisive yes or no must nevertheless come from us. It does not work any other way than that we be involved at the deepest levels with our own becoming. The fact that, to a large extent, man can 'thank himself' for his future being constitutes precisely the freedom of man in the universe.

What lives in us as unmastered and unpenetrated soul substance is the material, the construction material required to create the human being who wants to grow in us. It is not always easy to see what the blocks of stone waiting to be removed from a quarry will become — they must first be shaped. So too it is certainly not easy to see that something very different can be made out of the soul material represented by our instincts and passions, egotism and malice, doubts, despairs and fears.

Man is so profoundly entangled with evil precisely because he needs 'much material' for the construction of the future human being. This material has been made available through this, that the most precious forces have been 'enchanted' in three regions of our being (our discussion of sexuality is a good example). These forces are to be torn away from the grip of the Adversaries and returned to their own origin, but under the direction of the human being. In this way we will no longer be at the mercy of emotional compulsions, weaknesses and the decadence of life-forces, of suffering and frailty in the physical body, but we will be able to be Lord over the part of our being that is liberated and shapes itself creatively. Furthermore, with mastery over ourselves we will also achieve full authority over earthly and cosmic forces because we will have acquired a new relationship with the hierarchical beings in the spiritual world.

Certainly, this points to a vast programme for the future. Today we can only begin by transforming our soul body. We do not need to follow every wish, every instinct. Much can be achieved through self-education. In this region genuine transformations do take place, not only suppression and sublimation (refinement) of undesired soul-forces, of which there is much talk today in depth psychology. Friedrich Benesch, in his book on the *Apocalypse* says:

> In human soul life there is a difference between refinement
> and genuine transformation. Authentic transformation passes
> through sacrifice, death and resurrection. Refinement, known
> as sublimation in academic psychology, means that forces
> contained in the soul retain their original character, but appear
> in an apparently ennobled form.[3]

What we can achieve today in transforming our soul-forces is in an even more germinal stage in the realm of our life-forces and has hardly begun at all in our physical body. Nevertheless, there are beginnings in this realm too, which are above all connected with the turning to Christ described before. We observe transformation in the life body, for example, when someone takes their temper in hand and changes it in some measure. In the physical body it becomes perceptible, for example, in the spiritualization of the human countenance, which can occur over decades in a human life. However, we must bear in mind that we are dealing with enormous future developments, for which vast periods of time are required.

It will be essential for us to trust in the existence of such forces already within our being, which will continue to evolve and work within us throughout the future. On the inner battlefield of spiritual struggle to become a better person defeats remain numerous. The decisive element in our inner life is our *continued effort* to patiently work on the 'up-building' forces and not to give up despite the defeats. This is expressed in the following words of Rudolf Steiner:

> Man needs inner faithfulness.
> Faithfulness to the leadership of spiritual beings.
> Upon this faithfulness he can build
> His eternal being and character
> And thereby permeate, suffuse and strengthen
> The world of the senses
> With the spiritual forces of eternal light.[4]

The answer to all our failures is prayer, is for us to turn to the spiritual world and occupy ourselves with matters that lead beyond everyday life — without letting up. The voice in us that says, 'It doesn't really matter after all' definitely does not come from our good, higher self, but from Ahriman. On the other hand, Christ speaks to us words of peace and overcomes fear. He speaks to us of faith in the forces that will be available to us in the future, of trust in our future. Paul puts it this way:

> Not that I have already reached the aim or received the ultimate
> consecration. But I strive onwards on the path, so as to take
> hold of that for which Christ Jesus took hold of me. Dear
> brothers, I do really not think that I have achieved it. But one
> thing I may say: what is behind me is forgotten; my whole
> being stretches out towards what lies before me. My whole
> striving is for the prize that I see: the call from the heavenly
> heights to become one with Christ. (Phil.3:12–14 JM)

Part Three

Destiny and Evil

CHAPTER 14

Evil in the Evolution of Mankind

We have mentioned repeatedly that the Adversaries' influence on the history of mankind has undergone an evolution. The Luciferic and Ahrimanic powers have not always approached humans with the same power. Only gradually have they been allowed to attack with their full power, or we could also say that humanity has only gradually become receptive to their full effect while the Adversaries have become increasingly evil. This may become a little clearer if we consider individual biography. A child is still protected from many things by itself and by its environment. Only when he awakens, becomes independent and enters the surrounding world will he gradually be exposed to its dangers and temptations. Now he must have his own experiences in this area, go astray and stumble. All of this is an absolutely necessary part of the maturation process.

Certain ages play a role in this process. We know that the process of separation and becoming independent sets in around the third year. The child learns to say, 'I,' a period of defiance brings the will to manifest and assert itself. Articulated in countless questions the first conscious steps towards knowledge appear. Additional steps in development occur around the sixth and seventh years (school readiness) and the ninth and tenth years (inner separation from authority). The crisis during puberty is especially noticeable. It signifies a great deal more than physical maturation; it takes hold of and transforms the entire bodily-soul-spiritual being of the young person. Young people now often begin to withdraw from parental supervision and go their own way. It lies in the nature of our time that many things enter the lives of teenagers today that actually belong to a later stage of life.

Puberty is a decisive, but not the last, step in the individual's encounter with evil. For *full* responsibility for one's actions accrues to a person only between the twenty-eighth and thirty-fifth years. Correspondingly, temptation and dangers become greater. By those years we usually stand independently in our professional and personal lives. Our actions affect a greater circle of people; a wrong decision, or wrong lever pulled in a factory may unleash inestimable misfortune. A wrong step in one's personal life can destroy one's family and continue to work destructively in other social areas. Placed in such positions of responsibility an individual can experience the abyss of evil.

Progression of the Fall into sin

This sketch of the evolution of evil in the biography of an individual can help us understand its progression in the evolution of humanity. For here too we are dealing with an intensification of evil. We could call it the progressive Fall into sin.

Christa Meves has compared biblical scenes of the Fall into sin with the psychological development of the child and interpreted them as stages of development, the negative aspects of which match the positive aspects of maturation.[1]

The Fall into sin is an actual event that took place in the past. It falls in the middle of the period of time Rudolf Steiner called the 'Lemurian,' which corresponds to the end of the Paleozoic era. With this event, human beings began to separate from the realm of the divine and 'fall' to the earth. The sequence of incarnations in earthly bodies began. Only now did man really enter into experience of the earth.

The Luciferic influence drew the Ahrimanic into its wake. Ahrimanic powers saw to it that human beings not only walked on the earth, but also learned to own it. Humans took charge of the earth. The egotism stimulated by Lucifer — in a radical dedication to the earth — now became earthly power and striving for ownership of earthly things. Ahriman showed himself to be the 'Father of Lies', of deception, as he began to convince humans that earthly happiness is the one and only true value.

After the era of the Fall came a time, the age of ancient Atlantis, when humanity still had memories of the 'golden age' — we would speak of 'paradise.' Nevertheless, human evolution continued to lead humanity away from paradise. The Atlantean age extended through long ages. Its end was brought about by a catastrophe caused by the fact that Ahrimanic powers got the upper hand in certain areas of Atlantean culture. Atlantis went under due to a great flood.

The time after the flood

We find an echo of these events in the biblical tale of Noah and the flood. Here too anthroposophy can confirm the kernel of truth in this story. One of the greatest leaders of mankind, who can also be called an initiate, the biblical Noah prepared the rescue of the most advanced peoples at the end of Atlantis.[2] He saved them from the catastrophe and led them east, towards Asia in order to found a 'post-Atlantean' culture. Ultimately, all human culture of our era and the near future goes back to this deed.

The beginning of the post-Atlantean age was set in the ninth millennia before Christ. That is, at the end of the Pleistocene ice age. What began then was not simply a continuation of Atlantean conditions, in which human beings were still quite childlike, corresponding to the seventh to ninth years in an individual's biography, this new age represented a mighty further step on humanity's path: humanity began to awaken to the earth.

At first people still lived predominantly in groups formed around blood ties. The family, and tribal connections carried the 'I', *the individual's sense of self*, which was still very weak, in a way similar to how the 'I' had been carried in the spiritual world. Lucifer had freed it from the realm of the spirit; however, in the earthly realm it had to be sustained by banding together at first with other souls in a 'group soul,' similar to the way a child must first be carried by a family. In this way, Atlantean conditions continued working in post-Atlantean times. (And even up to the present day in some regions of the world we find family ties that prevent a person from becoming free.)

During the post-Atlantean cultures that followed, the Luciferic and Ahrimanic influences were already strongly present but were held back from unfolding their full impact by the forces of good; this was true for the Ahrimanic powers for a longer time than the Luciferic. Developing humanity was still partially protected, just as an individual human being is protected during middle childhood between seven and fourteen.

The *education* of mankind for the earth was at work in the first millennia of the post-Atlantean age — until the Egyptian culture. Just as a child is educated so that he can become a capable person on earth so too the spiritual leadership gave humanity an education for its path on earth. This education began at the start of the post-Atlantean age through Noah (also known as Manu in other traditions) and then continued through the millennia. Such education emanated from the mystery centres, which gave critical cultural impulses through the initiates that taught there.

Individual initiates, who at that time generally remained hidden within the mystery centres stepped forth to guide whole civilizations. Zarathustra, for example, gave powerful impulses to the ancient Persian peoples. He introduced the plough as a tool in agriculture and taught worship of the sun god. Other initiate teachers were Menes-Hermes in Egypt, Moses for Israel, Orpheus in Greece. The ideas and impulses that emanated from the mystery centres and their initiates were intended to give a maturing humanity adequate capabilities for descent to the earth, without allowing humans to lose their connection with the spirit too quickly. The new religious institutions and rituals were designed to preserve the connection with the divine.

Nevertheless, this connection was only possible to a certain extent; as time passed the connection grew weaker. The Fall into sin continued working as the negative influence of Lucifer and Ahriman also continued. A rich clairvoyance maintained the connection to the spiritual world during the Atlantean and early post-Atlantean times. Based on the body, this clairvoyance was possible while human bodies were still soft and plastic as is the case with a small child. A last, real experience of the divine-spiritual world was given in imaginations and visions, in powerful intimations and in 'true' dreaming.

However, this clairvoyance increasingly dimmed. Bodies became harder and denser under the influence of Ahriman; vision of the supersensible was extinguished. Even in the mysteries the possibility of being educated to a full experience of the spiritual world through spiritual exercises and initiation deteriorated over time. At the time of Christ, most mystery centres had already become non-functioning or even decadent. This was an inevitable development in the course of history. Increasingly, humans had to find their own way on earth.

When the time was fulfilled

Towards the end of pre-Christian times, approximately five hundred years before Christ, we find the intensified working of the Adversaries and spiritual vision slowly extinguishing. With this loss of vision two new abilities appeared: firstly, the ability to think independently and with that the beginning of philosophy, above all in Greece; secondly, simultaneously with this capability the free, self-responsible 'I' became a force to be reckoned with. This new impact of the self would not have been possible without independent thinking.

In Greece and Rome we see the seed for this capacity for independent thinking, which continued evolving in the Renaissance and is fully developed in our time. The fruit of the Fall into sin and Lucifer's ongoing influence showed itself fully in the age of the Greeks. Man had lost his original connection to the divine, he was 'free' from God, left to his own devices, but not free of Lucifer. And he found within the power to take hold of himself and determine his own fate, the power of thinking. At first this thinking is under the influence of Lucifer, as is the 'I' also. Yet there are forces within this power of thought, which, when properly taken hold of by consciousness, can lead beyond this influence.

Lucifer is at work in the development of the 'I' and thinking as they appear, freed for the first time in the age of the ancient Greeks. The entire, magnificent culture of the ancient Greeks carries the stamp of Lucifer's influence. Rome, with its solid connection to the earth and focus on earthly power, shows more the work of Ahriman. The magnificence of Greek culture, that advanced humanity so much, can show us how Luciferic powers are entirely placed in the service of evolution. In this sense Lucifer must serve us.

Yet there is great risk in all this. If man does not overcome from within the egotism trickling into him, then the beneficial effect of coming to himself will be superceded by the danger of becoming trapped within himself. He then makes himself into 'the measure of all things,' (an expression coined by the Greeks) because of his grotesquely intensified sense of self, and thereby loses any meaningful relationship to the world, indeed, to his true self. An integral part of the Greek cultural achievement, this danger soon belonged to all western civilization and in our time, to all mankind.

This point of view casts a new light on the Christ event. We have mentioned that the great initiates were at work giving new impulses to the various post-Atlantean cultures. Now at the 'turning point of time' something new appeared. Christ himself, who was not a leader of mankind nor an initiate, but rather originated in the divine world as 'the son God,' entered into the realm of mankind, which had lost the divine. The descent of Christ when the time was fulfilled, was the counterpole to man's Fall to earth.

In his booklet, *The Essence of Christianity*, Rudolf Frieling points out that it is not an accident that the expression concerning the 'fulfilment' of time appears in the Gospel. Why, one must ask, did Christ not appear much earlier for the healing and salvation of humanity? Wouldn't he have been able to help countless more people if he had come earlier?

This question can really be answered only in light of mankind's evolution of the self. There could have been a 'too early' for this development; namely, if the human 'I' had not yet awakened to freedom and independence by the time Christ came, or if Christ had come earlier then, because of the power of his divine presence on earth, which they would have perceived with their clairvoyance, humans would have fallen back into their old, childlike condition lacking any 'I'-consciousness, a condition they had been just about to grow out of.

Christ was not recognized by most people who met him. This shows precisely that the 'time was fulfilled.' Now he can be found only by those who freely recognize him, not by means of their ancient clairvoyance and knowledge but through the free power of love in their hearts. They were not overwhelmed by the power of his divinity. They could remain *themselves* and yet through him spiritually grow beyond themselves — to their *true* selves.

Christ could now come, but he also had to plant a seed in at least a few people, a seed that would turn Lucifer's deed to good. A new, free relationship to the divine had to be instilled, at least in a few human beings. This is a relationship that does not extinguish the 'I', the human self, that has become independent through Lucifer, but rather fills it with selflessness, opens it, so to speak, to a higher content.

With the exception of Judas, such a relationship had started with the disciples. John was able to make the most progress. In his Gospel we find the words of Christ: 'You in me — I in you.' (John 14:20). And Paul could say: 'Not I, but Christ in me.' The power to heal the deed of Lucifer, namely the temptation into egotism, lies in these words.

Renaissance and the present: increasing evil

The evolution and unfolding of evil certainly did not stop with the coming of Christ. To begin with, we note a mighty intensification of evil at the beginning of the twentieth century. This is connected with the fact that the Ahrimanic powers, set lose from the previous restraints holding them back, are now allowed to interfere, not only in the physical and life bodies, as previously described, but also in human *consciousness* with their full power.

The fifteenth and sixteenth centuries saw not only the arrival of the Renaissance Man, so ably portrayed by Martin Luther with his self-expression and self-assertion — as can be seen in the words ascribed to him 'Here *I* stand — *I* cannot do otherwise. God help *me!*' (three of the ten words stress the self), but also a *radical* turning of human attention to the earth based on a changed consciousness. This new attention then leads to exploitation of the earth, which again is only possible with the help of thought directed towards pure utility.

A far-reaching change in the nature of thinking can be noted at the beginning of the Renaissance. Rudolf Steiner speaks of a further Fall, an '*intellectual Fall into sin*,' brought about by Ahrimanic influence, the consequences of which are now fully visible in our time. The human capacity for knowledge is the fruit of the Luciferic influence; at first it was still developed in connection with the ancient, constantly less-certain clairvoyant vision in humanity. Ancient knowledge was, above all, clairvoyant knowledge; it had to be extinguished as mankind became increasingly earthly.

However, the ability, the power to know was not extinguished. It continued working. It no longer appeared as the capacity for imaginative pictures and inspirations, that were simply given to human beings from the spiritual world. It appeared, rather, as the power of independent thought, the contents of which were no longer received from outside, but rather 'self thought.' They had to be brought forward by the 'I' at work in self-consciousness, not in pictures and inspirations, but in thoughts. The development of philosophy, which did not exist until then, began.

As such, Lucifer had accomplished the decisive step: the 'uncoupling' of humanity from the guidance of the spiritual world. Paradoxically, this provided the leverage point, with the help of which human beings can fee themselves not only from the good side of the spiritual world, but also from the Adversaries. Lucifer himself supplies the sword for his overcoming. Expressed in words we have used earlier: the sickness itself provides the medication needed for its healing. For free, independent thinking is, since its development in Greece, the instrument with which the human being can take hold of himself. In thinking lies the starting point, through which alone we can take a position for ourselves and the world that is free — that is conscious and therefore self-responsible. With it we can also find the free will to turn back to the spiritual world. If the instrument of thought is unusable then this unique ability is in great danger. It is no wonder that the Adversaries apply their greatest force in this area.

We stand, therefore, at a second decisive stage of the history of the Fall into sin, with the further development of thought at the beginning of the Renaissance. The first stage was brought about by Lucifer in the 'first Fall into sin.' The second stage of the Fall has been taking place since the beginning of the Renaissance and continues in our time. This Fall is brought about by Ahriman who seeks to convince us that the earthly alone is real and uses this deception to place human thinking, which in itself is not at all earthly in its true nature, into chains. Ahriman has been almost completely successful with this deception. We can follow how, since the beginning of the Renaissance, philosophers and others have become increasingly uncertain when thinking about the spiritual world, to the point of completely denying anything spiritual in materialism. We can see in this something like a counterblow to the development of clairvoyant knowledge of ancient times. Knowledge in ancient times was almost entirely of the spiritual world with little interest in the earthly. Now the turn to the earth is complete. But Ahriman is co-opting our interest in the earth for himself and is extinguishing all knowledge of the spiritual world.

The consequences of this whole development are undeniable. Man can no longer recognize himself as a 'citizen of two worlds;' he knows himself only as a citizen of the earth. As such, he has become power-hungry and an egotistical hedonist who exploits everything earthly. The greatest powers of intelligence and the hard work of countless humans are offered up to create a complicated technology that has no higher purpose than to serve human comfort and entertainment, while simultaneously endangering all life on earth. In our surrounding civilization we see how, with the help of technology, this way of thinking leads to the creation of its own world. The idea of an Ahrimanic civilization presented here must not be equated with a rejection of modern life. Of course, we all participate in the achievements of this civilization and enjoy them. However, this development also presents us with new questions because our lives and the life of the earth is threatened. Here the radical rejection of some of the possibilities offered by a hypertrophied technology will be necessary.

In general, however, the rejection of 'the Ahrimanic' will not lead us into the future. What *will* lead us is the question: what strengths do we need to *develop* in order to meet the challenge facing us in this field? Connected with that is the question: must this second stage of the 'Fall into sin history' be seen only in a negative way, or can a positive aspect be found?

The captivation of thought, the tying of knowledge to the earthly gradually began at the start of the Renaissance. Before that there was no talk of limiting human thought to knowledge of the earthly, the visible alone. Plato and Aristotle, Plotinus and Augustine, Scotus Erigena and Thomas Aquinas bear witness to this fact. Of course, the spiritual world could no longer be seen by them in detail but *its existence* could still be thought. This tradition continued up to the beginning of the nineteenth century in the appearance of German idealism with Fichte, Schelling, Hegel, Goethe and Schiller.

But the knowledge that limits itself to the purely 'material' has succeeded magnificently and now has enormous momentum. This limitation put on knowledge was finally — apparently — confirmed and justified in the results of scientific research and in the philosophy of Kant. Kant proclaimed as a philosopher the absolute limits to human knowledge; he declared that humans are fundamentally incapable of any knowledge beyond the physical sensible world (which, according to Kant, also lacks objective truth) and that natural science can succeed without soul, spirit or God. When the French mathematician and philosopher, Laplace, was asked by Napoleon about the creator of our planetary system, he answered: 'This hypothesis I do not need.' And the famous nineteenth-century pathologist, Virchow, said, 'I have researched the entire human body — I have not found a soul.'

Following all this man has become a purely earthly being: an advanced animal; in his wishes and longings ruled by the unconscious; determined by heredity and environment; accidentally and without meaning thrown into existence; banished to a star that is nothing more than a dust particle in the gigantic universe that came from a big bang and will end just as meaninglessly as other stars before; no meaning and no God; no ultimate responsibility; no ideals and no love which are nothing more than illusions. The picture of the world resulting from Ahriman's inspirations. Have we been abandoned by God?

To the best of my knowledge, the spiritual science of Rudolf Steiner contains the only worldview that has the power truly to shake the world picture just described to its foundations, and in doing so to overcome the devastating feelings about life it creates. It can do this because it is based on comprehensive, understandable knowledge of the supersensary world. In anthroposophy one can find the liberation of human knowledge from its captivation by the earthly, and the one-sided extremes of all previous knowledge can be overcome. I am not speaking of a one-sided kind of knowledge directed only to the spiritual (clairvoyance) or a knowledge directed only to the earthly (intellectual) but a kind of knowing that can include both spiritual and earthly while showing how the two are interrelated. This is expressed in the verse already quoted in the first chapter:

> Seek the truly practical, material life,
> But seek it in such a way that it does not
> Numb your experience of the spirit that is active in that life.
> Seek the spirit, but do not seek it in
> Supersensible pleasure fed by supersensible egotism.
> But rather seek it because you want
> To apply it selflessly in a practical life in the material world.[3]

Anthroposophy is not limited to observing spiritual facts but rather wishes to show their connection to earthly facts. Some approaches to the spirit world turn their backs on the earth and seek to ascend into the spiritual world. Not this kind of knowledge. Anthroposophy can continue to contribute more and more in the future to the spiritualization of the earth just because it unites the two.

We have seen how in the past great leaders of mankind have given guidance and instruction that could work as an 'antidote' to Luciferic temptations. Today the remedy for the Ahrimanic darkening of our consciousness is present in anthroposophy and in the renewed rituals of the Christian Community. Whether or not they are actually used is, of course, left entirely to the freedom of the individual, who alone is responsible for his actions. The remedy is no longer collectively effective as in the past. It is present, however, and can show its fruitfulness in all areas of modern life.

How will it continue? Have the forces of Ahriman already achieved their high point?

The Antichrist

In the New Testament in the First and Second Letters of John, in Chapter 13 of Mark and, above all, in the Book of Revelation (Chapter 13), certain images of future events are connected with the appearance of the Antichrist, and with the direct intervention of the Adversaries into the world of earth. Rudolf Steiner also speaks about the various aspects of the Antichrist. It is clear from the Revelation of John that this intervention of the Adversaries does not represent the actual end of the world, but rather a necessary phase of its development. The present day view of 'The Last Days' usually errs in equating three things: the increase in strife and human problems, the second coming of Christ, and the end of the world. This mistake occurs in traditional theology but also in many religious sects, such as Jehovah's Witnesses. In view of future cycles of time, we must bear in mind that this equating of three different events is wrong. Even in the Gospel (e.g. Luke 21) increasing strife and human difficulties and the appearance of Christ in no way indicate the end of the world, although they contain the seed for the end. Here again the words from the Gospel apply: 'The hour is coming and is already here.' It alludes to a dynamic conception of time.

The appearance of the Antichrist does refer to a real future event, the awareness of which is of extraordinary significance for the present. This is because the preparations for this event directly concern us. In our time, humanity has matured enough to take on an even stronger attack from the Adversaries — just as mature adults are faced with greater dangers.

Ahriman is increasing his efforts to draw humanity to himself. The influence of Ahriman's power, which has penetrated human consciousness and thinking, is to be intensified to such a point that we can plainly speak of an 'incarnation of Ahriman;' Ahriman will be working directly through an earthly human being.

This event will have great significance for humanity, not only in a negative sense, but also in a positive one. Through the danger that confronts us from this event, positive forces within humanity will also be called forth; our task will be to work with those forces. In order to do this, however, there must be an awareness of the fact and the significance of this event. It must be clear that preparations for it are in full swing.

Rudolf Steiner described the following as preparation for Ahriman's incarnation:

1. Abstract thinking, the mathematical-mechanical view of the world, increasingly predominates; at the same time any spiritual understand of the world and man is lost.
2. The spiritual is 'preserved' in libraries, instead of being carried further in a living way and developed further. (Today we can think of the use of computers for every kind of knowledge.)
3. Faith in numbers (statistics) spreads and leads to all kinds of manipulation.
4. People will increasingly act without genuine interest in their actions. Not being able to be enthusiastic about spiritual ideas leads to apathy in one's public and personal life.
5. Disharmony in groups of human beings, partisanship, nationalistic impulses will increasingly fragment humanity.
6. A materialistic interpretation of the Gospel will lead to a false conception of Christ and to distorted visions of Christ.
7. There will be schools or training programmes that will, indeed, make people clairvoyant, but will not lead to objective visions of the spiritual world. This is clairvoyance in the sense of hallucinations.

These remarks by Rudolf Steiner confront us with the background of our age. Many people can sense them, and they must be seen through. Then the events that are being prepared for today will not be a terrible catastrophe, but a challenge to develop so much more powerfully the positive forces in human beings and to increase spiritual work. If knowledge about future events combines with such a will, then although they cannot be prevented, these events will have the value within human evolution that they must have.

The timing for these events falls into the third millennium, in 'the not too distant future.' As we approach these events there will doubtless be many severe conflicts in the foreground of world events. There will certainly be great efforts on the part of the Adversaries to make more or less impossible any real spiritual work in all areas of culture including religion. The signs of this happening can be seen everywhere.

But good forces opposing this are also present. The appearance of the Antichrist is being prepared in a sevenfold way, as described above. If we think of the positive side of these seven facts we have before us, at the same time, the antidotes, with which this event can be directed into the proper channels.

The appearance of 'objective' evil in our time is connected with the growing influence of Ahriman in human evolution and the preparations for his incarnation.

When tanks were introduced onto the field of battle during the First World War, a new chapter in the history of warfare began. People suddenly saw themselves confronted by a force against which personal initiative and courage were powerless. The age of 'material battles' had begun.

This is something of an archetype for much of what confronts us in today's world as superhuman evil, as evil separated from human beings. Indeed, in the face of such evil, all that individuals can do amounts to nothing. We are no longer dealing with evil that comes from human beings, which works, so to speak, from 'I' to 'I'. Evil is appearing anonymously, institutionalized, as official, bureaucratic, technical 'machinery,' which, like a tank, threatens to roll over everything human. Almost all areas of human existence today are permeated by this evil. This anonymous and objective evil has already become a worldwide threat in the danger of a nuclear catastrophe or even a nuclear war .

Clearly, all of this signifies a challenge to mankind such as we have never before seen. Previous means of fighting evil prove to be powerless and clumsy. A renewal of *all* aspects of human life, even into political, economic and social structures will be necessary to counter this evil. This too is a task not only for the next few decades but also for the next centuries. And this task will have to be taken in hand by mankind under great duress during tumultuous times.

However, the ideas necessary for this undertaking already exist in outline form. Rudolf Steiner developed them in 1919 as *The Threefold Social Organism*.[4] Using these ideas will make it possible finally to overcome the antagonisms that otherwise always lead to tensions and conflicts of war between peoples and nations. In the future it will be possible to form the life of humanity in such a way that a community of people can come about which includes every kind of diversity.

Naturally, the question arises whether we still have time to bring about the necessary development in humanity? Should we not fear that before we have time for all these changes a catastrophe might make all further life on earth impossible?

Outlook

In Lessing's book, *The Education of the Human Race*, he lists tasks yet to be accomplished. In the destiny of individual humans trials and critical moments occur, which are to bring us further along our inner path. Mastering them makes us more mature human beings. The same principle holds true for mankind as a whole.

In the time of ancient Greece the human 'I' was given the seed for its independence. At the beginning of the Renaissance this seed was developed to a certain degree: 'Here I stand, I' (Luther). This growth and evolution of the 'I' is clearly continuing into our time. Today it is so far advanced that it has led to isolation and loneliness for many people. Old ties (families, professional groups, religious communities) are no longer enough to give people a sense of belonging, so great has the individualization power of the self become.

The Luciferically-inspired development of the 'I' has reached the point where it is already pointing to something beyond itself: man has arrived at himself, but now he must experience the profound truth that he is not enough for himself. He must recognize that the world and other people belong to him and that he creates great misfortune if he persists in his own being.

We have already sketched a picture of man and how he stands in the world. An endless amount has been invested in human beings which will emerge only in the future. However, this emergence requires a provocation, a challenge from evil to bring it out. Such challenges come to humanity 'step-wise' in tasks to be mastered that will bring forth the good that lives in us.

Rudolf Steiner called the task given to us today and in the near future the encounter with *evil*. This encounter with evil is to reach its high point in the incarnation of Ahriman. It is not the result of an accidental sequence of historical events but rather a necessary development in human evolution, and is connected with the intentions of the spiritual leadership of mankind.

The Gospel also alludes to the deeper necessity for such events. Hence, we read of the difficulties connected with the reappearance of Christ: 'It is necessary for all this to happen.' (Luke 21:5–7) and Matthew and Mark add: 'Yet these are just the birth-pangs of a new world' (Matt.24:8; Mark 13:8).

It is not an accident that the image of labour pains is used here, pains signifying that something new and future-orientated wants to be born. In this picture we can understand the meaning of our age, also the meaning of the pain and difficulties that live in our time. As with a birth the pain alone has no meaning, but only becomes meaningful through the fact that it helps something from the future to break through.

We have not come to the end of human evolution. New capacities and possibilities will accrue to us out of what has been invested in us. This requires the pain, the labour pains that are beginning in our time.

CHAPTER 15

Michael's Battle and the Reappearance
of Christ

In mankind and its evolution we see a progression of the Fall into
sin and a powerful intensification of evil. In all this there is a challenge to humanity to bring to birth the potential for good that lies
within it. We need to see the suffering of our time as the labour
pains of such a birth. Are there helpers for this birth? Is heaven
watching without doing anything while mankind struggles with the
abyss?

The fall of the dragon

The Apocalypse of John portrays Michael as the leading Archangel
who throws the adversary powers out of the spiritual world and down
to the earth among human beings at a specific time (Rev.12). What
we have already considered from the earthly side — that Ahrimanic
powers are allowed to increase their effectiveness today even up to an
appearance of the Adversary among humanity — appears here from
the heavenly side. Spiritual deeds, the actions of the spiritual beings
play into all of human history on the earth.

The picture of the battle with the dragon and its plunge to earth is
confirmed by anthroposophy; even the timing of this event is disclosed.
A 'fall of the spirits of darkness,' occurred according to Rudolf Steiner
in the second half of the nineteenth century and concluded in 1879
with Michael's victory.

The spread of materialism on earth resulted from this event, for
there are two things connected with it.

Firstly, the intensification of evil on the earth is the consequence of
Michael's deed. In the pictures in the Apocalypse this evil appears as
the dragon, who is surrounded by 'his' angels. It is said of him that,

'he seethes with raging fury, for he knows that his time is only short' (Rev.12:12). The hectic stress of time in our age can be heard in these words.

The growth of evil has then a heavenly cause. Evil has changed its location. It no longer sends only its effects into humanity but is increasingly actually present itself. Among human beings this presence of evil appears at first as a darkening of consciousness and a capturing of thoughts, then as a realization of these dark thoughts, which finally lead to a threat to all life on earth. The spiritual beings cast down by Michael live in this threat. Human thought and action becomes destructive.

Secondly, the other side is that a new situation has arisen in the spiritual world. It has become free of the powers, which until then had 'darkened heaven.' Not only the world of demons, but also the world of heaven has acquired a new relationship to human existence. This, too, is mirrored by many facts of the present:

— in a new longing for spiritual truths, for meditation, for a spiritual way of life that has appeared in many people today;

— in a newly-arisen sense of responsibility for one's actions on earth;

— in the possibilities for an active involvement in many branches of life that have been renewed by knowledge of the spirit (pedagogy, work with the developmentally disabled, art, medicine, agriculture, etc.);

— in the truths of anthroposophy that are being revealed;

— and, not least, in the renewal of the religious life in the work of the Christian Community.

A river of spiritual life has opened up in the twentieth century and will continue to flow into the future. The spiritual world is beginning to live again among human beings in this river. When the spiritual horizon of Michael was swept clean, spiritual forces could awaken in human consciousness — at least in a delicate, inchoate way. But they will lead to increasingly clear thoughts.

It is Michael himself, standing directly on the threshold of human consciousness that leads to the spiritual world, who brings spiritual forces to mankind. He seeks to open the doors to the spiritual world again; he wants to continue his battle on the field of human consciousness against the forces of darkness and the enslavement of thinking.

The search for answers that countless people are involved in today is permeated by these facts. Everywhere today it is a question of new access to the spiritual world. Rudolf Steiner expresses this in the following verse.

> Where outer senses' knowledge ends,
> There and there only is the gateway
> That leads to the realities of life.
> The soul itself creates the key
> When it grows strong in the battle
> Which spiritual powers wage with human forces
> On the soul's own ground
> When the soul, through its own free will,
> Drives out the sleep, which
> At the senses' limits
> Envelops its capacity for knowledge
> With the darkness of spiritual night.[1]

When Michael opened the gateway to the spiritual world he had to cast the spirits of darkness down to the earth simultaneously. Here they are becoming a growing threat but also a continuing incentive for mankind to see good.

On the one hand, the forces connected to death and destruction are strengthened, 'charged up;' the depravity of human beings, such as Hitler, Stalin, Pol Pot, appears stronger and finds expression in taking hold of entire peoples. On the other hand, the spiritual world approaches and sends its forces into individuals. The higher selves of many are very active.

This creates great tensions — anxiety-filled, questioning, doubting *and* also hope-filled stress. Perhaps never before in the history of mankind has the human being been so hotly contested as today. And the spiritual world has never been so close to us as it is today since the Fall. Basically all of this is connected to the Second Coming of Christ. Christendom has, since the beginning, spoken about this event that will be fulfilled in our time and will continue into the future.

The Second Coming of Christ

Michael's deed is also a preparation for the Second Coming of Christ. Michael had to cleanse the realm of the spirit that borders directly on the human realm from the Adversary's power, in order to prepare the way for Christ to approach humanity again. From this spiritual place that is so close to human beings Christ can be experienced and also seen in the spirit, only by individuals to begin with, then by increasingly larger numbers of people and groups of people. We have already mentioned this fact, but only from the human side. Now we see it from the perspective of Christ. Through suffering, humanity is becoming mature enough to experience Christ's closeness. Christ, from his side, feeling the suffering of humanity, is taking a step towards us. Out of compassion for suffering mankind Christ is sending forth love that is so much more powerful, which becomes a bridge to every individual human heart. This is the deepest and greatest mystery of our time.

In this way, Christ has come very close to us. In an endless, loving and merciful way he is living with the destinies of all human souls alive today. He is waiting until the souls of individuals achieve the maturity needed to see him.

Why doesn't he simply become visible again? Why did he withdraw from human perception anyway? Wouldn't everything have been very different if he could have guided mankind's' fate through his presence?

We have already considered this question. Christ's ongoing presence would have made people unfree. The presence of God, if it is perceived in its fullness, has something overwhelming. For this reason, forty days after Easter, *Ascension* had to occur. Several people, the disciples whose circle was soon expanded to become the first congregations, had, indeed, taken up the seed of Christ's presence. But mankind as a whole was not able to endure his presence. Only today is the human 'I' slowly acquiring the maturity that enables it to take into itself what can stream forth from Christ. Through the experience of Christ's presence all human existence on earth will undergo a far-reaching transformation.

This perspective changes our view of the present and the future as well as our view of the work of evil, in two ways: We can understand the intensification of evil in our time more deeply if we recognize it as the despairing attempt by Ahriman to oppose the effectiveness of Christ's power. There can be no doubt that this is a serious threat for mankind. However, if we always see only what threatens, then we are subject to illusion just as much as if we made light of the threat. We only see the whole picture when we bear in mind that, on the balance-scale of mankind's history, although evil lies on one side, on the other balance-pan lies the destiny of God, who has united anew with humanity. This picture should work in our souls awakening us to our responsibility. Then the fears will slowly be transformed into courage and initiative to do what every individual can do wherever he or she may stand in life.

Furthermore, the spiritual world has ways of preventing what must not be. If the spiritual leadership of mankind does not want catastrophes of vast extent to occur, they will not happen. To be sure, this will also depend on human behaviour. There is no excuse for sitting back and doing nothing; whatever can be done to reduce threats of all kinds, must be done. What is crucial for the spiritual beings who lead humanity is whether they see enough strength and energy for the future in us, or if perhaps human selfishness threatens to draw us into the abyss.

The first case gives the angelic beings forces with which they can work to preserve us from ruin. In the second case it will perhaps not be possible to avoid catastrophes. For then painful disasters would represent the only means to protect us from falling into the abyss of darkness and soul-crippling selfishness. Such catastrophes might be the only way to make a new beginning possible.

It is impossible to comprehend the pain that would accompany such events. The full energy of every human being who considers such things must be directed today towards strengthening spiritual life on the earth, and working against the threats wherever it is sensible and possible. Then no doubt God will prevent what will not benefit mankind.

That Christ himself has united with humanity and the earth is the strongest support for this thought: the forces that preserve and carry us further come from him. Remembering this will not lull us into a false sense of security but will help to strengthen our sense of responsibility. It can reduce the fear that only weakens our strength.

What appears in the Old Testament as the destiny of the individual, Job, is coming true today as the destiny for the entire human race. Yet the increase in evil is not a hopeless tragedy or an abandonment by God. It represents, as with the destiny of Job, a higher trust from the side of God, that in the battle with evil mankind will acquire the strength to bring it to a relationship with the spiritual world that is no longer merely traditional: to an experience and vision of Christ's presence.

This new relationship has one meaning: if mankind finds its way out of bourgeois complacency and pleasure seeking, out of its irresponsible dealings with the earth, out of the illusory world of intellectual and materialistic worldviews, then it will find paths to a spirit-filled future — perhaps as Job did through pain and suffering.

At the end of his struggle Job is elevated to a higher state of being and also granted deeper insight into the mysteries of the universe. Because of this insight he becomes aware of his own origin within divine creation and can see himself not only as an earthly being, but also in his cosmic dimension:

> Have you entered into the springs of the sea,
> or walked in the recesses of the deep? ...
> Have you comprehended the expanse of the earth?
> Declare, if you know all this. ...
> *You know, for you were born then,*
> *And the number of your days is great!*
> (Job 38:16,18,21 RSV)

The work of the two Adversaries in creation is revealed to him in the figures of Behemoth and Leviathan. God shows him that both powers are *necessary* for the world to progress.

If we think of Job's destiny as having expanded today to include all of mankind, then not only is there the promise of a new experience of Christ's presence, but also a promise that we will be granted new insight into the mysteries of creation. We will understand the relationships governing the earth, the universe and God's creation, including the Adversaries' role. With the appearance of Christ, a light will fall, not only on the Adversaries, on their work in creation and mankind, but, above all, we will be able to see how the human soul is connected to the God who is continually working in all ages of the world. We will see the hierarchical beings united with God and all his work.

This will present us with new possibilities and capabilities because the experience of the spiritual world, of the presence and help of the angels and higher spiritual beings will change our lives, even in everyday details. From this experience we will receive entirely new strength and energy, new sources of inspiration even for practical action. So too a new light will fall on the meaning of evil which makes visible new ways of combating evil. All of this represents for us the future that is to be found in the event of Christ's reappearance.

How can God allow suffering?

Despite all that has been said concerning the meaning of evil, and in light of all the human suffering in the last century, the question will rise up in the human heart again and again: if all these things can happen, can I still believe in God?

Countless people have lost their faith because they are unable to feel that human want and suffering can be combined with the existence of God. Does evil still have any meaning when it is driven to such extremes? When it is carried so far can it still be included in God's plan for the world? Is this all really necessary for mankind's path?

We can really only answer this question with 'yes' out of the infinite depths of Christianity, out of the being of Christ who encompasses all humanity. Every answer that does not consider the profound significance of Christ's sacrifice must appear superficial. What does it mean that Christ gave himself to humanity through his sacrifice? And what does it mean that he is uniting himself even more deeply with humanity through his 'Second Coming,' today? If we think of these statements not as beautiful clichés, but as simple statements of fact, then our view changes. Then these facts mean that Christ has united with those human beings who are suffering, not with those who are comfortably situated.

It was not for nothing that he says the words, 'what you have neglected to do for the least of my brothers, you failed to do for me.' (Matt.25:45 JM) Wherever a human being is suffering, Christ is suffering with him or her. Wherever a cross has been put up for a human being, it has also been put up for Christ!

In view of these facts, we can grasp the essence of Christianity. It is not a new teaching; it is a deed, a sacrifice of Christ in his devotion to mankind. What Job divined, that man has an advocate in the heights, that a saviour lives, has become an earthly reality in Christ. God does not reside in heavenly separation far from humanity. He is really, truly suffering with his creatures. He unites with every single human being, also in his or her need, loneliness and pain, both in soul and body.

We must feel and grasp the reality of Christ's closeness if we wish to have a true picture of Christ. The cross of Christ himself always arises anew in the cross of humanity. But this also means that with every cross carried by a human being since Golgotha, the power of resurrection is also given.

Is God allowed to intervene? Would he not put into question the entire meaning of world evolution if he were to free us from evil with a single, simple divine act? Would that not remove the possibility of our fighting through to liberation ourselves? God trusts in the endless possibilities and powers that have been placed in humans. Should he not know us, he who created us, in the very depths of our souls? Shouldn't he know what can be expected of us?

We would perhaps not dare to speak in this way were it not for the experiences reported by so many who have survived the terrible suffering of the present and recent past. The descriptions of Jacques Lusseyran come to mind as well as the death-experiences in German concentration camps, which led to an experience of higher life; or similar stories from the well-known physician, Victor E. Frankl; or the experiences that Mihailo Mihailov collected from Russian camps, just to mention a few. In all these experiences we can see that in the encounter with radical evil the deepest spiritual forces in man are called forth.

Mihailov says, out of his experience in the eastern concentration camps:

> That they had to endure under conditions of imprisonment the worst psychic and physical torture, but at the same time they also experienced moments of perfect happiness such as would be unimaginable for people outside the walls of the camp ... accordingly, the external lack of freedom could also be defined as extremely concentrated, intensive life ... one is reminded of a world by Berdyayev that it is not man, but God who wants man to be free.[2]

These experiences bear witness to the fact that in the challenges brought by evil, deeper, otherwise hidden forces in the human being can be awakened and taken hold of. Fairy tales also show this truth, for example in 'The Devil with the Three Golden Hairs,' in the descent to evil the courageous one acquires something that could not be acquired in any other way. It is then available to him as a force that leads him further: the power of the higher, creative good.

The higher good

Let us compare the goodness of a child with that of a mature older person. In the behaviour of the child, as wonderful as it may appear in certain moments, there is not yet anything that can stand on its own, nothing permeated by the personality of the individual. In the best sense of the word, it is impersonal, having flowed forth directly from the world's spring of goodness. In large measure the child in his goodness is dependent upon the goodness of his environment that makes it possible for the child to be good — he simply mirrors his environment. If he is brought into a bad environment with deleterious influences he cannot maintain his good will, but must take up something from the environment into his behaviour.

With an adult we speak not only of goodness but also of kindness. One can perhaps say that kindness is not only a condition, a state of being, but rather something creative — kindness sends something out into the world; it brings forth goodness in an ongoing way. It is not a reflection of the surrounding world, but creates the world surrounding it. It is something achieved by individual humans, often by consciously living through many great and painful experiences, something that comes forth entirely out of the core of their personality.

We are describing something wonderful that can flow forth from the maturity of the human soul. It is a power that is entirely personal because it can only be created by the most personal experiences in one's destiny. And yet it does not seek itself. As kindness it would like to provide comfort, help, harmony and positive, up-building forces for other people. The most inner aspect of a person strives outwards bestowing creative forces on others. We see in this fact the stirrings of what we can call the divine forces placed in man.

We can imagine the pattern found in individual development from childhood to maturity on a larger scale for the development of mankind as a whole. Indeed, all the forces that lie in a human being can be seen on the larger scale of all humanity. In the beginning, mankind lived from the forces streaming into it from the surrounding spiritual and earthly worlds. The last remnants of such conditions can be found today in the so-called primitive tribes, which, to a large extent, are still bound to the physical and spiritual in nature.

However, mankind has been striving on its path of evolution towards another condition where, in essential aspects of its existence — spiritual and even material — it is no longer dependent on its environment and does not reflect this environment. It is a condition in which mankind *creates* its environment and is able to give *other* beings and worlds the possibility of existence, in much the same way in which the kindness of an individual affects others. The substance of the divine that was placed in human beings in the beginning (indicated by the biblical words: image and likeness of God) is to flow forth and become 'creative of worlds' *from the core of the human being*, as something achieved by the individual self which is permeated by the individual personality. The words of the Act of Consecration of Man that speak of love that is creative of being, through which the good will endure, point to this future goal.

In this sense, we can speak of a higher good that is not only a 'being good,' but actually a creative power, which as a human power will create and shape the world of the future out of the inner depths of man, and will unite humans and humanity with God in a new, independent way. 'You are gods' — we may be shocked by these words but they were spoken by Christ (John 10) in order to illuminate the future of mankind.

The seed of resurrection

In light of the endless depths asleep in the human being waiting to be awakened, we can begin to grasp that these deep possibilities must be set in motion by the immense power of evil — just as many of the greatest creative achievements in mankind's history were often 'called forth' by extraordinary difficult destinies. Nevertheless, we must once again ask: does it have to be that way? Isn't God acting carelessly when he lets all this happen to humanity?

This question would certainly be justified if God left us all alone exposed to evil. But this is not the case. God unites with our suffering. Christ in us is suffering with us. He is suffering our pain out of an all-encompassing kindness that exceeds human capacity. In this kindness he is present in every human pain and human suffering, even the deepest and the darkest.

One day we will recognize that what we have suffered, he has suffered in his closeness to us; really, truly suffered. But as Christ really feels the pain with us he is also carrying it out of endless kindness. He did not reject it, he let it work within him so that the kindness of his being, the creative good could stream forth from him.

What does the presence of Christ in all suffering mean? It means that he can plant, in every individual's suffering, the power to overcome it. We can find this power in him. Already now, but certainly in a later era we will be able to recognize him in our pain as he helps us to overcome it. We will learn from him to extract higher life and the power of resurrection from suffering and death. So the question, 'how can God allow that?' opens our eyes for a higher light that can fall on the riddle of suffering and evil.

Christ is walking alongside us through our destiny. He does not force us to notice his presence. But later — perhaps only after death — we will recognize him in his deep connection to our personal destiny. Step for step in the after-death survey of our earthly life he will show us that the deepest suffering can call forth the greatest good, that we also have the power to find this greatest good.

The question of God's allowing evil looks very different from this perspective: God is not sitting on a throne in the heights of heaven looking down and judging us, but rather through Christ God is suffering with us, in order to place a seed for the power of resurrection in every suffering, in every pain. We can freely take hold of this seed when we turn to Christ. So understood, experiences at the limits of human suffering — by Lusseyram, Frankl, and Mihailov, among others — become experiences of Christ and at the same time are experiences of the power of the greatest creative good that belongs to man.

CHAPTER 16

The Overcoming and Redemption of Evil: Questions for the Future

Mankind has not been left alone with evil. It is true that God has not removed the burden of evil for he does not want to rob us of the incentive to create good. Nevertheless, we are not left alone. He has sent his *Son*, part of himself, who has united with all human suffering. Christ is also suffering whenever a human being is suffering, but he also plants the seed for resurrection and the overcoming in all suffering, which we must take hold of sooner or later when we mature enough to recognize Christ's presence. In this way divine help — we also call it grace — and respect for human freedom work together.

Christ and evil

Until now the attention of Christianity was always directed to overcoming death through Christ. It was easy to overlook the fact that a second victory was achieved through the suffering and death of Christ: the overcoming of evil. For our age, this second deed is perhaps more important. Christ released *higher life* out of death. By overcoming *evil* he awakened the beginning of a *higher good*.

In the events of his passion we see Christ not only walking towards death, we also see him suffering terrible pain. In the violence of inhuman destruction and gruesome aggression evil approaches him unveiled. The scourging and the crucifixion are among the most horrible forms of martyrdom that can be inflicted to a body. We need to bear in mind that Christ really felt and carried this pain. It is not as though, because he lived as a divine being in his body, he were somehow above the pain. On the contrary, because he was equipped with a divine capacity for experience he had to feel the pain more intensely than an ordinary man.

Christ lived through the deepest human suffering. Hence, he looked the power of evil full in the face. *Externally*, there were human beings standing in front of him during those experiences: the man Jesus, the soldiers and deputies. *Inwardly* the divine power of Christ is standing over and against the power of evil working through men, evil that showed its face in the raging features of humans. For the first time since the separation at the beginning, the eyes of God looked again, directly and unveiled, into the eyes of those beings, who, since that original separation had to live distanced from God. The Temptation (Matt.4) was a first step towards this, the actual confrontation.

Without a doubt, there was nothing in the eyes of Christ other than love — not love of evil, but love of the ground of existence which was still present even in the utmost evil. The ray of this love met the inner soul of those beings now facing him. Can what happened even be measured?

What happened when Christ stepped in front of evil's power of death, Ahriman himself, and their eyes met? What happened when the highest love rayed into the heart of the Adversary? Is this not precisely Christ's struggle with the powers of hate and death that he brought them his love and they had to withdraw and turn from this love? We can imagine perhaps how not only a seed for the overcoming but also for the redemption of evil was planted.

Richard Wagner touches on this mystery in his opera *Parsifal*. He portrays Kundry, who must serve evil, in an earlier life on earth encountering the Christ as he carries his cross towards Golgotha; she laughs at his pain: 'His gaze met mine.' This 'look' that Christ gave her pursues her and will not let her alone. She finally finds redemption in her encounter with Parsifal. The seed of this redemption had been given to her in the gaze of Christ.

What Christ has lived before us in this way should find its continuation in the way individual human beings live their Christianity: overcoming evil through good.

Christians and evil

In the First Letter of Peter we find some poignant remarks concerning this theme:

> For a human being is raised above himself when he is able to
> endure suffering in the awareness of being in the sight of God,
> and especially so when he suffers without having deserved it.
> For what is special about enduring the blows which you have
> earned by your failings? But when you have done the Good
> and then patiently accept what you have to suffer: that raises
> you above yourselves before the countenance of God. For to
> this you have been called, for did not Christ also suffer for
> you? Thus he has given you his example and the way you can
> follow in his steps. His deeds were without sin, no false word
> came from his mouth. When he was reviled, he did not revile
> in return. His suffering forced no word of bitterness from him.
> (1Pet.2:19–23 JM)

And later in chapter 3, verse 9, he says: 'Do not repay evil with evil and insult with insult but rather bless; for you have been called in order that you may pass on the power of blessing.' (JM)

Everywhere evil meets the power of blessing, the seed that Christ planted through his patient endurance to overcome evil, this seed of transformation continues working. What is important above all is that we carry our own personal destiny with patience just as Christ 'took up his own cross.' But we also see him confronting the money changers in the Temple with a whip, confronting lies and injustice with punishing words of reprimand.

We find *both* attitudes in him: He took Judas into his circle of disciples, he promised the criminal on the cross next to him (Luke 23:43), he forgave the adulteress (John 8), according to his words both the good and the bad were granted admittance to the hall of the King (parable in Matt.22), he recognized the power of Caesar *in his proper realm* (coin for tax in Matt.22:15). This characteristic is found in all the Gospels. However, when it is the right thing to do his words have a cutting edge, his deeds have the power to judge.

So the situations we may find ourselves in demand an active intervention for good. Not to prevent evil when it is possible would itself be an injustice, but to do this requires two things: knowledge concerning evil, that is, the ability to not confuse evil with good; and the power, when rebuking evil, not to become evil oneself — raging with anger, filled with hate, emotional — that means to preserve the power to bless.

Can we imagine Christ filled with hate when he encountered his enemies? Indeed, it was precisely the love that emanated from him that made him unconquerable. If he had hated then the hate would have taken possession of him. Evil cannot be overcome with evil, only with good. In following Christ, mankind is called upon to intensify the power of good and to overcome, yes even transform, evil. According to Peter, Christians have to 'pass on the power of blessing.'

We recognize the same approach that we described for our inner life, only here applied to the external world: it is better to 'build up' the good in oneself than to constantly engage in battle with evil, battles that one usually loses.

Certainly, one who can prevent a murder will do that; anything else would be injustice, but would he have to devote his life to fighting crime? Perhaps as a good teacher, doctor, pastor and altogether a good contemporary he might be able to prevent more murders, through his daily actions than in any other way. This does not mean to say anything against the absolute necessity for fighting crime, and the need for the sacrifice of those people who devote their lives to fighting crime.

Innocent peacefulness acquired by avoiding all controversy can certainly never be a Christian goal. What can be an ideal for us in this regard is expressed in the Sermon on the Mount: 'Blessed are those who bring peace into the world for they will be called sons of God' (Matt.5:9). This speaks of an active force in us to spread peace. It is not sufficient to demand, to long for peace. The question is: what am I myself doing daily to bring peace into the world? The question of peace is *ultimately* directed to us as individuals.

Someone once said: 'Everyone would like to have peace but very few are prepared to do what creates peace.' As long as we expect peace from others, we ourselves will find no peace. Only when we are prepared, in ourselves and around us, to do everything that creates peace will we accomplish something real for peace and also for humanity.

The armour of God

It is clear that earth is the place of conflict. We do not seek the earth as humans in order to enjoy a comfortable life. Taking the initiative for good — as we have seen in the example of Christ — also means battle. Paul even speaks of the armour of the spirit, which should be available to Christians (Eph.6:11–17). He speaks of a sword but it is the 'sword of the spirit,' something very different from the 'sword' of our emotions, our hate, our self-seeking which would be closer at hand. He speaks also of the 'breastplate of righteousness,' by which Paul means the ability to place oneself in the world in a way that is spiritually justified.

Along with the 'helmet of salvation,' the 'shield of faith,' 'girded about the loins with truth,' all of which is *spiritual* armour, the 'shoes' are also mentioned, which are 'prepared to spread the gospel of peace.' Here the power to create peace is brought together with the feet, with which we 'step' on the earth. This picture can only mean that the power of peace can stream through human beings so powerfully that our path becomes a 'path of peace,' as is stated in Luke 1:79, and then our steps no longer darken the earth but pacify it.

The earth is the place of conflict and battle. The question is — what are our weapons and what are we fighting for? If we are 'fighting for peace' (a contradiction in itself) and are only increasing self-seeking and hate in the world then we will have fought only for war. Then we will have only increased the demons of war and there will certainly be no peace. It is a great illusion to believe that evil could be destroyed or exterminated through any kind of external measures. The opposite is the case, for evil is a spiritual thing and spiritually effective. Only spiritual weapons, as Paul refers to them — faith, righteousness, truth, peace, etc. — will have any effect here.

We will not be able so soon to prevent battles, both inner and outer, but *how* we stand in them, depends on us. What we will increasingly need is something of the spiritual armour of Christ. When Christ confronted his Adversaries there was nothing in him except love. Peter's words 'you have been called in order that you may pass on the power of blessing' do not mean a lame and lazy peacefulness but an active creating of peace, especially when stepping forward for good.

Love evil into the good

These words from Christian Morgenstern in one of his poems could be called a Manichaean ideal for the future. In his poem, Morgenstern says:

> Be a brother to all!
> Help all, serve all
> Is, since HE appeared
> the only Goal!
>
> Even the scoundrel
> who strives against us!
> He too was once
> woven of light
>
> 'Love evil into the Good!'
> the deepest souls teach us.
> Learn to steel the
> courage of love with hate
>
> 'Brother' — Hear the word!
> That it become truth
> And one day the earth become the place of God![1]

There are attitudes expressed in this poem that we have seen before. They are not far from Peter's words, 'Do not repay evil with evil and insult with insult but rather bless: for you have been called in order that you may pass on the power of blessing.' (1Pet.3:9 JM) And they are much like the words of Christ when he speaks of loving not only your neighbour but also your enemy. 'Love your enemies, pray for your persecutors' (Matt.6:45).

What do we mean with the term 'Manichaean ideal for the future'? A great impulse for the future is connected with the figure of Mani, who appeared in the third century as an important founder of Christian churches. His teachings were violently suppressed because his contemporaries misunderstood them. Mani was put to death in a way that was accompanied by terrible suffering, a horrible encounter with evil. This encounter with evil prepared him to contribute something to the overcoming of evil in the future. Rudolf Steiner said:

According to the Manicheans evil is an integral part of the cosmos. It contributes to the evolution of the cosmos and in the end must be absorbed and transformed by the good. The great, unique mission of the Manicheans is to study the meaning of good and evil, of joy and pain in the world.[2]

Elsewhere, in looking at the future, he says:

Then good and evil will form an entirely different opposition than today ... In those people, whose karma has resulted in an excess of evil, evil will especially step forward in the spiritual. On the one side there will be human beings present having a mighty inner goodness, kindness, geniuses of love and kindness. On the other side the opposite will also be present. Evil will be present as an attitude uncloaked in a large number of human beings, no longer disguised, no longer hidden. The evil people will celebrate evil as something especially valuable ... Today we are standing immediately before an age when a conscious conflict between evil confronted by the good will occur ... [the future] will have the task of drawing evil through kindness into the flowing stream of evolution again as much as possible. A spiritual stream will have arisen that does not strive against evil despite the fact that evil will appear in the world in its demonic form. The consciousness will have grown strong that evil must again be drawn into evolution, but that it cannot be overcome through battle but only through kindness.

On the one hand, therefore, the development of evil will become more radical in some human beings. Against this, however, the power to overcome and transform evil will also grow to an unimaginable extent. Mani will be involved in all of this in an integral way. What we said concerning the power of blessing, and what may appear as illusory for our time, will be powerfully developed in the future. There will be a 'magic of love' that does not coerce but is able to dissolve the coercion of evil and create even more good.

All that will be the fruit of the fact that Christ not only experienced death but also evil and was able to plant the seed of redemption towards the higher good in evil itself.

Redemption of evil?

After all that has been said the question could now arise: if the origin of the Adversaries is to be seen as a development of the hierarchies then is it perhaps possible that they could be led back to their 'rightful' place in the spiritual world?

Only from this perspective do we have a complete view of the riddle of evil and its relationship to man. Indeed, it is unthinkable that higher members of the hierarchies who became evil could be lost in eternity. A seed for the redemption of evil was planted in the deed of Christ, but humanity is to participate in this process. With the forces of good acquired through the struggle with evil together with Christ, mankind is to lead the Adversaries back into the ranks of the angels, from which they were torn to help with the evolution of humanity.

With this thought we are touching on an idea that was not alien to early Christianity: Origenes, one of the most important church teachers of the third century spoke of the 'Restoration of all Beings.' He attached it to words found in Acts of the Apostles (3:21) in a speech held by Peter, and united with this the conviction that there was to be a restoration of all, even the fallen beings, into the harmony of God at the end of time. He expressly included Satan (*De Principiis* 1.6 and 3.6) His teachings were later declared heretical by the established Church. The conception of eternal damnation completely blocked the path to thinking that for all sinners and even for the devil an ultimate reconciliation might be possible. The authorities felt that the punishment of sin would appear less severe if it did not last for eternity.

In one of the most important works of the middle ages, Dante's *Divine Comedy*, the conviction that the punishments of hell will last for eternity is portrayed in drastically dramatic pictures. We encounter in this book the mercilessness, which belonged to the old dogma of the damnation of souls. In seven increasingly dark circles, Dante describes the abyss of eternal hell as endless torture and horror. The pictures, drawn with excruciating, graphic vividness, increase in horror each step down. One can imagine that such images containing so much graphic vividness had to be impressed into human souls for a time in order to make clear the unfathomable depth of evil. Today, however, it is high time for the idea of the restoration of all beings to take the place of the idea that the tortures of hell last for eternity.

Of course, there appear to be passages in the New Testament that contradict this, for example, the report of 'eternal' fire, etc., (e.g. Matt.18:8; Mark 9:43–47). Are these passages not speaking about the 'eternity' of torture after death? We must bear in mind here that the Greek word used in the New Testament *aíon* (aeon) means something very different from our word 'eternity.' Our abstract concept of eternity would not even have been understood in ancient times. Back then people would have had to attach concrete temporal rhythms, 'cycles of time,' or 'era' in the sense of a large but limited expanse of time. Hence, it was possible to speak of a present and a future 'aeon.' 'Aeon' did not mean 'eternal' but rather a region of being, 'cycle of time,' having various qualities. The future aeon had a higher quality compared to the present.

These linguistic considerations make it very doubtful that the New Testament passages cited contained our concept of eternity. After death human beings experience everything they have ever caused another person to feel, as if they were the person receiving their own actions. All joy but also, and perhaps most importantly, all pain and injustice we cause others come back to us after death. We live in it and it feels like fire that cannot be extinguished by any external source. We are forced to endure this, and we are also willing to suffer this after death because it gives us unimaginable depths of self-knowledge, indeed, until our soul has been purged of the corresponding inclinations (either towards selfish actions that injure others or towards the sensual aspect of earth that has no place in the spiritual world), that is, until the fire burns out. This fire does not burn eternally; but it has a different quality from earthly fire. This other quality is called 'aeonic.'

We do not wish to downplay the seriousness of the afterlife experiences described here and their far-reaching effect on humans. However, they have nothing to do with an 'eternity' of hellish punishment.

One can ask further, in this vein, about the pictures appearing at the end of the Apocalypse. Here too we read about the drastic suffering of those who find themselves excluded from the further evolution of the earth. The word 'eternal' or 'eternity' appears in the Apocalypse only in connection with the Gospel and the Godhead itself, when it speaks of the 'eternal [aeonic] Gospel,' or of the 'aeon of aeons' of the Godhead. We must read very carefully here. There is a description of how the suffering of those excluded from evolution 'rises' 'in the aeons of the aeons.' This does not mean 'for ever and ever' but rather 'in the region of progressing cycles of worlds and rhythms of time' (Rev.14:11; 19:3; 20:10). What was said above concerning the 'fire after death' appears here magnified as an apocalyptic picture for the epoch 'after earth,' as a picture for an even deeper-reaching fire of purification that must be endured by those who have consciously permeated themselves with evil. In this process the duration of the fire is significantly longer, but again, nothing like 'eternity' in the modern sense is intended. These expressions mean rather the long-lasting rhythms of time (cycles of time), in which God lives, but above all, they mean the different 'quality' in which the purification of evil occurs.

The pictures themselves already point beyond. For how are we to imagine the 'blessedness' of mankind if the 'smoke' of the suffering of those left behind rises into this 'blessedness' and darkens it in a horrible way? (Rev.19:3). Isn't it easy to think that those humans who have advanced will still be doing all they possibly can to bring about release and redemption?

Again, in saying this we do not mean to take anything away from the seriousness of the decisions coming at the end of time. They will definitely have a quality of inexorable hardness and tragedy to begin with, that is an 'aeon long,' but must they prevail for 'eternity?' At the Last Supper, didn't Christ still give the bread to Judas before his betrayal, as a pledge towards future forgiveness and redemption?

The attitude behind Dante's descriptions is remote to us today. We experience too clearly how difficult it is to have to bear the compensation for all the evil, for all the errors of humans. But the idea that pain and misery, despair and disintegration, should rage in the soul for eternity, as an expression of God's justice, appears to us today not only as meaningless — for who would benefit from it — but also as not in keeping with God's mercy. If it is true that, in death, Christ descended not only to the realm of the dead, but also to hell in his 'Descent into hell,' as we are told by Christian tradition, only hinted at in the New Testament (1Pet.3:19; Eph.4:8–10) then we must be able to find a seed of overcoming and redemption in hell itself.

The pictures in the Apocalypse do not portray the end. They describe a phase of development, not the absolute end of the world. As we have seen, they point to something beyond themselves. For a time — like Dante's images — they are to impress humanity with the seriousness of evil; just as it was necessary for a time to stress the uniqueness of a single life on earth, as opposed to the truth of reincarnation.

Today we can expand our view in both realms, not in order to lose the seriousness of the situation, but in order not to despair. The 'last days' described in the Bible are not the end. A further rhythm of time leading beyond the descriptions in the Apocalypse will bring the possibility of the 'restoration of all things.' The biblical description is not inclusive or complete. It is open for additional stages in the future. The Apocalypse presents pictures of the end of earth's development. We have seen that the question of evil, which remains unsolved at the end of the Apocalypse, leads us beyond the end of the earth.

Origenes' thoughts concerning the 'restoration of all beings' includes evil itself. Also the adversary powers, who went through their descent for the sake of human beings, are to find their 'call home' and then just integration into a future cosmos of the spirit. We see a hint of such possibilities in the fairy tale where it says that the devil has a daughter, who is inclined to good.

The great world drama of the battle of evil powers against man and God does not lose any of its dangers and terror through such thoughts, but as humans we are drawn into a higher responsibility, for we are the reason why evil had to be developed. We are also the most deeply permeated by evil. If man in the future is really to develop the power intended for him then the possibility of redeeming evil will also be included. The circle of our deliberations is completed with this thought of man's highest calling. In the way portrayed here we can hope for an evolution of our human capacities precisely because of the stimulations from evil but with the help of Christ.

Nevertheless, the possibilities of individuals as *individuals* are exceeded here. For here is a task awaiting *mankind*. All the forces God has invested in humanity will have to work together in order to create a common power against the superhuman powers of the Adversaries. To do this, East and West will have to unite with the Middle in their highest and best qualities and possibilities. This means that the gifts that every culture and every people carry in terms of their unique spiritual forces and impulses must become universally human. That is a task for the distant future and yet it belongs to the wide perspective connected to the question of evil. It is this wide perspective that alone lets us imagine the great goal of the future: not only overcoming evil, but also transforming and redeeming it.

In concluding this book let it be said that I do not claim to have solved all the riddles of evil. I do hope I have shed light on important points by the use of new perspectives. The real solution to the riddle of evil is a question directed to the future of mankind and ultimately — because we ourselves are this future — a question directed to us.

Perhaps the points of view presented here will help to transform in our souls what always wants to oppress us as worry and fear. For fear itself, as we have seen, is the work of the Adversaries, just as other Adversaries would lead us to think that things aren't really so bad. We must practise courage and responsibility wherever we may stand on earth and in life — that alone is appropriate for the future. This book is intended as a contribution to such practice.

Further Reading

For a discussion of the evolution of consciousness and the different modes of feeling, conceptualizing and perceiving reality in the past, consult the following books:

Owen Barfield, *Saving the Appearances: A Study in Idolatry* (1957) Wesleyan University Press, Middletown, Conn, 1988.

Owen Barfield, History in English Words. (1926) Floris Books, Edinburgh, 1985.

Francis Cornford, *From Religion to Philosophy: A Study in the Origins of Western Speculation.* London: 1912. Peter Smith, Magnolia, Massachusetts, 1958.

Erich Neumann, *Origin and History of Consciousness.* Tr. R. F. Hull. Bollingen Series, Vol. 42. Princeton University Press, 1970.

Books by Rudolf Steiner:

Intuitive Thinking as a Spiritual Path: A Philosophy of Freedom, Translated from Vol. 4 of Collected Works, the German Gesamtausgabe (hereafter GA), Anthroposophic Press, Hudson, NY, 1995.

An Outline of Esoteric Science (GA 13), Anthroposophic Press, Hudson, NY, 1998.

Theosophy: An Introduction to the Spiritual Processes in Human Life and in the Cosmos (GA 9), Anthroposophic Press, Hudson, NY, 1994.

How to know Higher Worlds: A Modern Path of Initiation (GA 10), Anthroposophic Press, Hudson, NY, 1994.

Books by other authors:

Emil Bock, *The Apocalypse of Saint John*, Floris Books, Edinburgh, 1986.

—, *The Childhood of Jesus: The Unknown Years*, Floris Books, Edinburgh, 1998.

—, *Kings and Prophets: Saul, David, Solomon, Elijah, Jeremiah*, Floris Books, Edinburgh, 1988.

—, *Saint Paul: Life, Epistles and Teaching*, Floris Books, Edinburgh, 1989.

—, *The Three Years: The Life of Christ between Baptism and Ascension*, Floris Books, Edinburgh, 1980.

Evelyn Francis Capel, *Christ in the Old and New Testaments: Towards a New Theology*, Temple Lodge, London, 1989.

Rudolf Frieling, *Christianity and Reincarnation*, Floris Books, Edinburgh, 1974.

—, The Complete *New Testament Studies*, Floris Books, Edinburgh, 2021.

—, The Complete *Old Testament Studies*, Floris Books, Edinburgh, 2022.

—, *Hidden Treasure in the Psalms*, Floris Books, Edinburgh, 2015.

James H. Hindes, *Renewing Christianity*, Anthroposophic Press, 1995.

Hans-Werner Schroeder, *The Christian Creed: A Meditative Path*, Floris Books, Edinburgh, 1982.

Edward Reaugh Smith, *The Burning Bush: Rudolf Steiner, Anthroposophy and Holy Scriptures — An Anthroposophical Commentary on the Bible.* Anthroposophic Press, Hudson, NY, 1998.

—, *David's Question: "What is Man?"*, Anthroposophic Press, Hudson, NY, 2001.

—, *The Soul's Long Journey, How the Bible Reveals Reincarnation.* SteinerBooks, Great Barrington, MA, 2003.

Endnotes

Chapter 1

1. *Summa contra Gentiles*, III, 71.

2. 'Das Wesen des Gebetes,' in *Pfade der Seelenerlebnisse* (GA 58) Dornach, 1957.

Chapter 2

1. Chapter titled 'The evolution of the world and the Human Being' in Steiner's book *An Outline of Esoteric Science* (GA 13), in earlier editions titled: *Occult Science, An Outline*.

2. *Wahrspruchworte* (GA 40).

3. In some quarters today there is mention of a 'third' form of evil, evil beings which Rudolf Steiner mentioned on a few occasions: the so called 'Asuras.' Their work will unfold in the future. Today they are present only as 'indications,' so to speak, in germinal form under the 'cloak' of Ahrimanic powers. What is happening in the world today can be fully understood as an intensification of Ahrimanic influences. For this reason we will not be discussing this third form of evil in this book.

4. There is a discussion of this in chapter 6 of Steiner's book, *The Threshold of the Spiritual World* (GA 17), Anthroposophical Publishing Company, London, 1956.

5. Of course, this brief mention of the eastern (Asian) and western (American) approaches to life and the spirit does not do justice to these two regions. There is much that would need to be said if we had space to go into this question. Much can be found on this theme in Steiner's volume of lectures, *Polarities in the Evolution of Mankind* (GA 197), Rudolf Steiner Press, London, 1987.

Chapter 3

1. For a more complete description of these pictures and images that have been used in different myths at different times in the past to depict evil consult the German edition of this book.

2. Rudolf Meyer, *The Wisdom of Fairy Tales*, Floris Books, Edinburgh, 1988.

3. Mario Jacoby, Verena Kast and Ingrid Riedel, *Witches, Ogres and the Devil's Daughter, Encounters with Evil in Fairy Tales*, Shambala, Boston, 1992, p. 37.

4. ibid.

Chapter 4

1. For a detailed description of this topic see, Schroeder, Hans Werner, *Mensch und Engel* (Man and Angel), Verlag Urachhaus, Stuttgart, 1981.

2. *Dionysius the Areopagite. On the Divine Names and the Mystic Theology.* Tr, C.E. Rolt. The Macmillan Co, London, New York, 1920.

3. *An Outline of Esoteric Science* (GA 13), Anthroposophic Press, Hudson, NY, 1998.

Chapter 5

1. For a more complete discussion of how philosophers have dealt with the problem of evil see the German edition of this book.

2. Rudolf Steiner's *Second Mystery Drama*, 9th Scene.

3. Steiner, Rudolf. Lecture 10 and answer session in *The Spiritual Hierarchies and their Reflection in the Physical World. Bell's Pond Hudson* (GA 110), Anthroposophic Press, Hudson, NY, 1970.

4. Lecture 5 in Steiner, Rudolf, 1948, *The Gospel of St. John in its Relation to the Other Three Gospels, Particularly to the Gospel of St. Luke.* Anthroposophic Press, Hudson, NY.

Lecture 12 in Steiner, Rudolf, *Manifestations of Karmam* (GA 120), Rudolf Steiner Press, London, 1984.

5. Lecture 3 and 4 of Steiner, Rudolf, *Die Evolution vom Gesichtspunkte des Wahrhaftigen* (GA 132), Rudolf Steiner Verlag, Dornach, Switzerland, 1979.

6. ibid. Lecture 3.

Chapter 6

1. Jung, C.G., *Antwort auf Job*, Rascher Verlag, Zurich and Hamburg, 1961, p 31.

Chapter 7

1. From chapter titled 'The Soul World' in Steiner, Rudolf, *Theosophy: An Introduction to the Spiritual Processes in Human Life and in the Cosmos* (GA 9), Anthroposophic Press, Hudson, NY, 1994.

2. Lecture titled 'Das Böse im Lichte der Erkenntnis vom Geiste' (Evil in Light of Knowledge of the Spirit), in Steiner, Rudolf, *Geisteswissenschaft als Lebensgut* (Spiritual Science as Substance for Life) (GA 63), Rudolf Steiner Verlag, Dornach, 1959.

3. Görres, Albert Dr. Med. Et phil., Professor for Medical Psychology, Psychosomatic medicine and Psychotherapy, *Das Böse — Wege zu seiner Bewältigung in Psychotherapie und Christentum*, Freiburg, 1982.

4. Article 'Angst' (Fear) by Johannes Hoffmeister in *Wörterbuch der philosophischen Begriffe*, Hamburg, 1955.

5. Lecture on Aug. 8, 1951, in Steiner, Rudolf, *Menschenwerden, Weltenseele und Weltengeist* (Evolution of Man, the World and the Spirit) (GA 206), Rudolf Steiner Verlag, Dornach, 1967.

Lecture on Sept. 24, 1921, in Steiner, Rudolf, *Cosmosophy, v. 1*, (GA 207), Anthroposophic Press, Spring Valley, NY, 1985.

Lecture on Nov. 6, 1921, in Steiner, Rudolf, *Die Gestaltung des Menschen als Ergebnis kosmischer Wirkungen* (Forming the Human Being as the Result of Cosmic Workings) (GA 208), Rudolf Steiner Verlag, Dornach, 1956.

6. Lecture on Oct. 27, 1922, in Steiner, Rudolf, *Physiologisch-Therapeutisches auf Grundlage der Geisteswissenschaft II* (Physiological and Therapeutic Perspectives Based on Spiritual Science), (GA 314), Rudolf Steiner Verlag, Dornach, 1975.

Chapter 8

1. *Theosophy: An Introduction to the Spiritual Processes in Human Life and in the Cosmos* (GA 9), Anthroposophic Press, Hudson, NY, 1994.

2. Lecture 3 in Steiner, Rudolf, *The World of the Senses and the World of the Spirit*, Steiner Book Center, North Vancouver, B.C., Canada, 1979.

3. Grohmann, Gerbert, *The Plant, Volume II, Flowering Plants*, Bio-Dynamic Farming and Gardening Association, Kimberton, PA, 1989, p. 42.

Chapter 10

1. Steiner, Rudolf, *A Psychology of Body, Soul, and Spirit, Anthroposophy, Psycholophy, & Pneumatosophy*, Anthroposophic Press, Hudson, NY, 1999.

2. Görres, p. 41

3. Lecture 4 in Steiner, Rudolf, *Necessity and Freedom*, (GA 166), Anthroposophic Press, Hudson, NY, 1988.

4. Steiner, Rudolf, *How to know Higher Worlds: A Modern Path of Initiation* (GA 10), Anthroposophic Press, Hudson, NY, 1994.

Rittelmeyer, Friedrich, *Meditation: Letters on the Guidance of the Inner Life, According to the Gospel of St. John*, Floris Books, Edinburgh, 1983.

Schroeder, Hans-Werner, *The Christian Creed, A Meditative Path*, Edinburgh, Floris Books, 1982.

5. Fromm, Erich, *Die Seele des Menschen — Ihre Fähigkeit zum Guten und zum Bösen*, Stuttgart, 1980, p. 22.

6. Barz, Brigitte, *Festivals with Children*, Floris Books, Edinburgh, 1984.

Bock, Emil, *The Rhythm of the Christian Year, Renewing the Religious Cycle of Festivals*, Floris Books, Edinburgh, 2000.

7. See the introductory chapter in: Schroeder, Hans-Werner, *The Christian Creed — A Meditative Path,* Floris Books, Edinburgh, 1982.

8. Capel, Evelyn Francis and Ravetz, Tom, *Seven Sacraments in the Christian Community*, Floris Books, Edinburgh, 1999.

9. Lusseyran, Jacques, *And There Was Light*, 1963, Little Brown and Company / Floris Books, Edinburgh,1985.

10. Steiner, Rudolf, *Intuitive Thinking as a Spiritual Path: A Philosophy of Freedom* (GA 4), Anthroposophic Press, Hudson, NY, 1995.

Chapter 12

1. Leber, Stefan, *Geschlechtlichkeit und Erziehungsauftrag — Ziele und Grenzen der Geschlechtserziehung*, Freies Geistesleben, Stuttgart, 1981.

2. Lecture 13 in Steiner, Rudolf, *Theosophy of the Rosicrucians*.

Chapter 13

1. Steiner, Rudolf, *An Outline of Esoteric Science* (GA 13), Anthroposophic Press, Hudson, NY., 1998.

2. Lectures 8 and 12 in Steiner, Rudolf, *The Apocalypse of John* (GA 104).

3. Benesch, Friedrich, *Apokalypse, Die Verwandlung der Erde, Eine Okkulte Mineralogie*, Stuttgart, Urachhaus, 1981, p. 45.

4. Steiner, Rudolf, *Wahrspruchworte*, 1969, p. 262.

Chapter 14

1. Meves, Christa, 'Austreibung als Anstoß zur Reife,' in Illies, Joachim, *Die Sache mit dem Apfel*, Freiburg, 1972.

2. Bock, Emil, *Genesis: Creation and the Patriarchs*, Floris Books, Edinburgh, 1983.

3. Steiner, Rudolf, *Wahrspruchworte*, 1969, p. 262.

4. Steiner, Rudolf, *Towards Social Renewal* (GA 23), Steiner Press, London, 2000.

Chapter 15

1. Steiner, Rudolf, *Wahrspruchworte*, 1969, p. 105.

2. 'Die Erde — Ein Durchgangslager' in *Die Christengemeinschaft*, Jan 1976.

Chapter 16

1. Morgenstern, Christian, 'Bruder' in *Wir fanden einen Pfad*, Munich, 1914.

2. Lecture on May 26, 1906, in Steiner, Rudolf, *Kosmogonie* (GA 94).

Lecture on November 11, 1904, *Die Tempellegende* (GA 93)

Index

Floris Books

For news on all our **latest books,**
and to receive **exclusive discounts,**
join our mailing list at:

florisbooks.co.uk/signup

Plus subscribers get a FREE book
with every online order!

We will never pass your details to anyone else.